UNDER COVER

UNDER COVER

An Anthology of
Contemporary Scottish Writers

Edited by
Colin Nicholson

MAINSTREAM
PUBLISHING

EDINBURGH AND LONDON

First published in Great Britain in 1993 by
MAINSTREAM PUBLISHING COMPANY (EDINBURGH) LTD
7 Albany Street
Edinburgh EH1 3UG

ISBN 1 85158 548 6

A catalogue record for this book is available from the British Library

Typeset in Perpetua by Litho Link Ltd, Welshpool, Powys

Printed in Great Britain by The Cromwell Press, Melksham

Contents

Acknowledgments

'A Man in Assynt' by Norman MacCaig is from *Collected Poems*, published by Chatto & Windus; *Daft Dan* by Joan Lingard was first published by the *Scotsman*; *Houses and Small Labour Parties* by Alasdair Gray is from his collection *Ten Tales Tall and True*, to be published by Bloomsbury; 'The Great Famine' by Sorley MacLean is from *Somhairle: Dàin is Deilbh*, published by Acair; *Street-Sweeper* by James Kelman is from *The Burn*, published by Minerva; 'A Mother Worries' by Liz Lochhead is from *Dreaming Frankenstein and Collected Poems*, published by Polygon; *Bizarre Situations* by William Boyd is from *On the Yankee Station*, published by Penguin; *Mick's Day* by William McIlvanney is from *Walking Wounded*, published by Sceptre; *Armageddon* by Valerie Thornton is from *Meantime*, published by Polygon; 'Climacteric' by Alexander Hutchison is from *Deep-Tap Tree* published by University of Massachusetts Press; *Being Frank* by Ian Rankin is from *A Good Hanging*, published by Century; 'The Chair' by George Bruce is from *Interim*, published by University of Nevada Press. We gratefully acknowledge the respective publishers' permission to reproduce this material.

Preface

This book contains stories and poems by the famous and the not yet so famous who have freely donated their writing in honour of something special and significant: the twenty-fifth anniversary of Shelter in Scotland.

Some of the pieces here have been published before; again, many have not. Although diversity of content, style and language are one of the greatest pleasures of any anthology, this book has, I think, a particular coherence provided by the writers' shared commitment to Shelter and the superb job it does in facing up to the growing problems of homelessness.

Notwithstanding an honourable mention in the poem, 'Thursday Morning, in a Glasgow Post Office', our involvement in this book springs from a simple but deeply held belief: that the universal way in which The Post Office touches everyone's life in Scotland – the more so in the lives of the less-fortunate, perhaps – provides a natural stepping stone to modest support for Shelter in this anniversary year. We also hope an even more tentative association between those who carry letters and those who write literature will find favour.

We would wish all those who contributed to this book, and to Mainstream, the publisher, much satisfaction.

We would also wish Shelter congratulations for the past twenty-five years and every success for the future.

Above all, we wish to the many in need of shelter speedy comfort.

KENNETH GRAHAM
Chairman
Scottish Post Office Board

Foreword

Shelter started its work in Scotland twenty-five years ago. The task at that time was to persuade the public that despite the fact that local authorities had had an obligation to identify and meet housing needs in their area for the previous fifty years, homelessness and slum housing still blighted the lives of many in Scotland. Shelter was at the forefront in the campaign to draw attention to the inadequacy of the rights available for homeless families. This early work bore fruit in the Homeless Persons Act 1977. Part of the continuing work of Shelter has been to try to ensure that this legislation did not simply provide empty rights but that the community's treatment of those without adequate accommodation was 'civilised'.

The tasks facing Shelter over the past quarter of a century have altered as the policies of successive governments have sought to restrict the rules of government in housing. Shelter has campaigned vigorously to ensure that the policies adopted reflect the aspiration that decent housing at an affordable price in the right place is the right of all those in the community. This has involved working to influence central and local government policies. Shelter has also provided assistance, support and advice from its Housing Aid Centres to those in acute need, experiencing homelessness or facing eviction. The organisation also pioneered projects involving the provision of insulation, developing care and repair and self-build initiatives around Scotland. This work has stemmed from the recognition that while the problems facing those who are badly housed are many and various, the solutions required also need to demonstrate adaptability. It is with regret that those involved in this work have to acknowledge that much remains to be done. Shelter's vision and values are not universally accepted. There has been much excellent work done already; much remains still to be done.

The staff who have worked for Shelter in Scotland over the past twenty-five years have been the central reason for the success the organisation has enjoyed in this crucial work. Outstanding commitment and energy shown over the years has been a mark of Shelter workers. During my own involvement in Shelter's Scottish Advisory Council since 1980 I have also had the pleasure of working directly with outstanding directors who have been able to harness this expertise to develop the vision of Shelter. The way in which first Noel Dolan and then Martyn Evans responded to the situation facing the organisation was outstanding. On behalf of the Scottish Advisory Council I would like to take this opportunity to thank them and all those who have worked for Shelter in Scotland for their efforts on behalf of the homeless and badly housed in Scotland in the past twenty-five years.

We are immensely grateful to those who have contributed to this volume and who have donated their royalties to support the work of Shelter. As the contents page makes clear, we have been fortunate in obtaining the services of an outstanding collection of writers. Many thanks to the Post Office for their generous support, and to Colin Nicholson for making this possible.

PETER ROBSON
Chair of the Scottish
Advisory Committee
of Shelter (Scotland)

Mick's Day

WILLIAM MCILVANNEY

It is Tuesday, not that it matters. The calendar is what other people follow, like an observance Mick Haggerty used to practise but has lost faith in. For Mick, most days come anonymous, without distinguishing features of purpose or appointment.

In any week only one time has constant individuality: Monday when he goes to the Post Office to collect the money on his Social Security book. It is the only money he is ever guaranteed to have. Sometimes, in the pub, mainly on a Friday or a Saturday, an evening will enlarge into almost a kind of party, an echo of the times when he was earning. (Earlier this year, a local man home from Toronto, remembering Mick's generosity when he was working, and aware of how things are with him now, slipped him a tenner.) But there is no way to foretell these times. For the most part, the names of the days are irrelevant.

But this is Tuesday. He wakens and reckons the morning is fairly well on. Sleeping late is one way to postpone having to confront the day. Doing that means going to bed late so that he won't surface too early. This is not a room he likes to lie awake in. Its bleakness works on the mind like a battery for recharging your depression.

The permanently drawn curtains are admitting enough daylight to light the room. The wallpaper beside his bed shows the familiar patches of pink below the peeled sections of floral, landmarks for his conscious-ness. The floor is bare boards with one small piece of carpet on them. Besides the bed, the furniture is two chairs. One of them is a battered easy chair for holding his clothes. The other is a wickerwork chair on which the ashtray sits, with a week of ash and cigarette-stubs in it.

He has no cigarettes but that isn't important. He has developed an intermittent style of smoking. He occasionally buys a ten-pack of Benson and Hedges and usually only smokes if he is having a drink and some-times not even then. When he is offered a cigarette, he tends to alternate one acceptance with several refusals, perhaps maintaining his hold on a habit he can't well afford or perhaps measuring the charity he'll accept.

He gets up and dresses. He had thought of changing his shirt but the only clean one he has left is a green shirt someone gave him, and his Protestant origins in Feeney near Londonderry make him sometimes a little reluctant to put it on.

He goes through to the living-room where the only time-piece in the house, an old alarm clock, lies face-down on the mantelpiece. If you don't keep it lying face-down, it stops ticking. It is ten past ten. He looks into the other bedroom to check that Old Freddie is all right.

Old Freddie mutters vaguely in acknowledgment of his presence. Freddie is in his early seventies and he has had a rough night. He usually does on a Monday, for that is when Mick pays him his £8 rent from the Social Security money. Freddie can't handle the drink the way he used to. The operation that gave him a bag where his bladder should be can't be helping.

Mick comes back through to the living-room. Its furniture echoes the kind of furniture in the bedroom: bare floorboards with a few pieces of carpet, a battered sideboard and three beat-up chairs and a raddled settee. There is an old wireless. They had a second-hand television but it went on the blink.

They have lived in this house for a year now. Mick doesn't like it as much as the first house. He has had digs with Old Freddie for twelve years, ever since Mick's marriage broke up after sixteen years. 'It just didn't work,' Mick says. At least there were no children who would suffer. For about a year after that he lived in a Model Lodging House, long since demolished. Then Freddie offered him digs. For a time in the other house Freddie's sister lived with them. She was separated from her husband, a miner who had gone to Nottingham to look for work. Even after she rejoined her husband, the house seemed to retain a little of her touch. Mick feels that a house where there isn't a woman never gets to feel quite right.

He goes through to the kitchen. He and Freddie buy their food separately, keep it in separate cupboards. They find that is the best way to try and make the money last. But if either of them runs short of food, it is an agreement that he can share the other's. Mick makes himself two fried eggs, a slice of bread and butter and a cup of tea.

When he has eaten, he goes to the lavatory. He washes himself in cold water. He comes through to the living-room, puts on his jacket and collects his library books. He may go to the public library two or three times a week. Before leaving the house, he looks in on Old Freddie again.

Outside, it is cold but not raining. One of the bleakest urban prospects you will see is a run-down council housing-scheme. All such architecture ever has to commend it is freshness. When that goes, there is not the residual shabby impressiveness of Victorian buildings, like an old actor rather grandly down on his luck. There is only grey roughcast stained with weather, overgrown gardens, a flotsam of rubbish left when the tide of respectability receded.

Mick's street is mainly like that. The council has refurbished a few houses, adding red-brick porches to the front. But the majority of the houses are the architectural equivalent of a huddle of winos. Some have been boarded up. Grass grows through the flagstones of the pavement in some places. From the scale of the dog-turds that aren't uncommon on the pavement, it wouldn't take an Indian scout to work out that the dogs around here tend to come in big sizes. One or two can be seen almost at any time of the day, mooching vaguely around as now, as if they too were on the dole. A big black dog is reading the pavement with its nose. From time to time it lifts its leg and squirts like an aerosol, adding its own comment.

Mick is heading towards the park as his shortest way to the town centre. His route takes him past the rubble of a recently demolished block of old flats towards a vast empty area already cleared. Men appear to be testing the ground there, presumably for rebuilding. On his left is a lemonade-making factory not long shut down. A few of its windows are broken and a door hangs open. He knew three sisters not much younger than himself who never married and who had worked in that place since they left school.

Mick himself is fifty-seven now. It is four years since he's worked. There have been times, he says, when he could lose one job and find another in the same day. Since he came from Ireland to Glasgow (where he lived for three years) when he was eighteen, he has worked in a flour mill, in an engineering works, on hydro-electric schemes, but mainly in the building trade. He was proud of his reputation as a good worker. He was never given to saving, knowing there would always be another job. Then, four years ago, there wasn't. There still isn't. He should know, he says. He has been looking.

When he arrives at the pedestrian precinct in the town centre, he joins some men he knows who are lounging there. The desultory talk among them is about the horses and dogs and who's done what and to whom and where there might be a job going.

Mick wonders briefly about going along to the Job Centre and decides against it. It's a bit like having your own uselessness officially confirmed. He used to go there a lot but the regularity of failure becomes harder to take, not easier. And every year that passes makes work for him less likely. 'It's hard enough for men in their forties,' he says. 'They don't want you when you're my age.'

Mick leaves the men in the precinct and goes to the public library. There's a nice girl there who knows him by name now. His favourite books are detective stories and cowboy stories. But he reads more or less anything. One of the books he really enjoyed was by a man named Leonard Woolf. He thinks it was called *The Village in the Jungle*. Today he picks three cowboy books: *Max Brand's Best Western Stories, Trask and the Mark of Kane* and *Manhunter*.

When he comes out, the temptation is to go to the pub. But if he goes to the pub, the danger is that he will stay there, nursing pints till it closes. This is only Tuesday. If he exhausts his money now, it will be a long way to the next oasis. He walks back home.

Old Freddie is still in his bed. He isn't feeling talkative. Mick comes through to the living-room and starts half-heartedly reading *Max Brand's Best Western Stories*. He doesn't like reading so much during the day. His best time for reading is late at night and in the early hours of the morning. Old Freddie is coughing.

The drinking doesn't agree with Freddie any more, if it ever did. It is perhaps a good thing that he no longer has his redundancy money. When he was paid off, he was offered £30 a month or a small lump sum. Freddie chose the lump sum and had liquefied his assets, as it were, within a year. But he had some good nights.

Mick finally goes to the pub in late afternoon. The pub is the focal point of his life. It is companionship, unofficial social work department and cabaret. Everybody knows him. If he is struggling, quite a few people there are prepared to stand him a drink. It is an understandable indulgence because any time Mick has money he isn't against buying a drink for someone else.

In the pub, too, both the owners and the customers have been known to help Mick out. He may get a pub-meal for free. Someone may bring him in a winter anorak. He may get the offer of a few hours' gardening. It's that kind of pub, a talking shop rich in anecdote where most of the people who go are well known to one another. Perhaps people don't mind helping Mick because he is remarkably unself-pitying and unembittered about his situation. If he ever falls out with anyone, it is usually in a righteous case.

He has more than a touch of the Galahads in his nature. One night in the pub Mick saw a woman being annoyed by a man. Mick decided to administer chastisement. But the man unsportingly moved and Mick's fist connected with the woman's forehead: damsel in deeper distress. But she understood the chivalry of the intention and proceeded to wear the lump like a Burton diamond. (Perhaps the moral is that when a drunk Irishman comes to a lady's aid, her trouble may only be starting.)

Tonight Mick stays till the pub shuts and comes out mellow but not, he feels, drunk. There is in the park, between him and home, a flight of earth steps buttressed with wood. The height between steps is uneven. Mick is in the habit of using them to gauge his condition, like a blood sample. Tonight the alcohol count isn't high.

When he gets home, Freddie is in the living-room. He has eaten and gone out but he hasn't had much to drink. Mick makes himself toasted cheese on two slices of bread and a cup of tea. He usually eats more than he has eaten today, his favourite food being liver.

Freddie doesn't want anything but they sit and talk as Mick eats. They mention Freddie's sister, who died in Nottingham. They talk again about whether Mick will ever go back to Feeney. Mick can't see it happening, since he would hardly know anyone there any more.

When Freddie goes to bed, Mick picks up *Trask and the Mark of Kane*. The street is quiet. He hunkers down into his personal situation, bothering no one.

But the more time that passes like this, the less capable Mick is likely to become of ever getting out of his present helpless condition. Time never merely passes. It defines us as it goes until we run out of potential to contradict what it tells us. Mick's situation is like a prison sentence without any crime committed. It is an indeterminate sentence. So far he has served four years.

A Man in Assynt

NORMAN MACCAIG

Glaciers, grinding West, gouged out
these valleys, rasping the brown sandstone,
and left, on the hard rock below – the
ruffled foreland –
this frieze of mountains, filed
on the blue air – Stac Polly,
Cul Beag, Cul Mor, Suilven,
Canisp – a frieze and
a litany.

Who owns this landscape?
Has owning anything to do with love?
For it and I have a love-affair, so nearly human
we even have quarrels. –
When I intrude too confidently
it rebuffs me with a wind like a hand
or puts in my way
a quaking bog or a loch
where no loch should be. Or I turn stonily
away, refusing to notice
the rouged rocks, the mascara
under a dripping ledge, even
the tossed, the stony limbs waiting.

I can't pretend
it gets sick for me in my absence,
though I get
sick for it. Yet I love it
with special gratitude, since
it sends me no letters, is never

jealous and, expecting nothing
from me, gets nothing but
cigarette packets and footprints.

Who owns this landscape? –
The millionaire who bought it or
the poacher staggering downhill in the early morning
with a deer on his back?

Who possesses this landscape? –
The man who bought it or
I who am possessed by it?

False questions, for
this landscape is
masterless
and intractable in any terms
that are human.
It is docile only to the weather
and its indefatigable lieutenants –
wind, water and frost.
The wind whets the high ridges
and stunts silver birches and alders.
Rain falling down meets
springs gushing up –
they gather and carry down to the Minch
tons of sour soil, making bald
the bony scalp of Cul Mor. And frost
thrusts his hand in cracks and, clenching his fist,
bursts open the sandstone plates,
the armour of Suilven:
he bleeds stones down chutes and screes,
smelling of gunpowder.

Or has it come to this,
that this dying landscape belongs
to the dead, the crofters and fighters
and fishermen whose larochs
sink into the bracken
by Loch Assynt and Loch Crocach? –
to men trampled under the hoofs of sheep

and driven by deer to
the ends of the earth – to men whose loyalty
was so great it accepted their own betrayal
by their own chiefs and whose descendants now
are kept in their place
by English businessmen and the indifference
of a remote and ignorant government.

Where have they gone, the people
who lived between here and
Quinag, that tall
huddle of anvils that puffs out
two ravens into the blue and
looks down on the lochs of Stoer
where trout idle among reeds and
waterlilies – take one of them home
and smell, in a flower
the sepulchral smell of water.

Beyond Fewin lies the Veyatie Burn – fine
crossing place for deer, they trot over
with frills of water flouncing
at their knees. That water rests in Fewin
beneath the sandstone hulk
of Suilven, not knowing what's to come –
the clattering horserush down
the Kirkaig gorge, the sixty-foot
Falls . . . There are twenty-one pools
on the Kirkaig . . . Since
before empires were possible
till now, when so many have died
in their own dust,
the Kirkaig Falls have been walking backwards
twenty-one paces up their own stream.

Salmon lie
in each of the huge footprints.
You can try to catch them –
at a price.
The man whose generations of ancestors
fished this, their own river,

can catch them still –
at a price . . .

The salmon come from the sea. I watch
its waves thumping down their glossy arches in
a soup of sand, folding over from one
end of the bay to the other.
Sandpipers, ringed plover, turnstones
play tig with these waves that
pay no heed but laboriously get on with
playing their million-finger exercises on
the keyboard of the sand.

The salmon come from the sea. Men
go out on it. The *Valhalla*, the *Golden Emblem*
come in, smoking with gulls,
from the fishing grounds of the Minch
to lie, docile, by the Culag pier.
Beneath it the joppling water
shuffles its blues and greens till they almost
waver the burly baulks away.
From the tall bows ropes reach ashore
in languid arcs, till, through rings, round
bollards, they clot and
twist themselves in savage knots.
The boats lie still with a cargo
of fish and voyages.

Hard labour can relax.
The salty smell outside, which is made up
of brine and seaweed
and fish, reaches the pub door but
is refused admittance. Here,
men in huge jerseys drink small drinks.
The thick talk
of fishing and sheep is livened
by a witty crackle of gossip
and the bitter last tale
of local politics. At ten o'clock, the barman
will stop whistling a strathspey to shout
'Time, please!' and they

will noisily trail out, injecting a guff of alcohol
into the salty smell made up
of brine and seaweed
and fish, which stretches from the pub door
all the way to America.

Whom does the sea belong to?
Fat governments? Guillemots? Or men
who steal from it what they can
to support their dying acres?

Fish from the sea, for Glasgow, London,
Edinburgh. But the land, too, sells
itself; and from these places
come people tired of a new civilisation
to taste what's left
of an old one. They outnumber
the locals – a thing
too easy to do . . . In Lochinver,
Achmelvich, Clashnessie, Clachtoll
they exchange the tyranny of the clock
for the natural rhythm of day and
night and day and night and for
the natural decorum that binds together
the fishing grounds, crofting lands
and the rough sheepruns that hoist themselves
towards the hills. They meet the people
and are not rejected. In the sweating night
London and Edinburgh fall away
under the bouncing rhythms of *Strip the Willow*
and the *Gay Gordons*, and when the lights go out
and all the goodnights are spoken, they can hear
a drunk melodeon go without staggering
along the dark road.

But the night's not over. A twinkle of light
in Strathan, Brackloch, Inveruplan, shows
where the tales are growing round, tall
as the mast of the *Valhalla*, and songs are sung
by keeper, shepherd and fisherman,
each tilting his Rembrandt face in the light

and banging the chorus round, till, with a shout
he takes up his dram and drinks it down.
The Gauger of Dalmore lives again
in verses. An old song
makes history alive again,
as a rickle of stones people the dark theatre
of the mind with a shouting crowd and,
in the middle, MacLeod of Assynt and
his greater prisoner – Montrose.

An old song. A rickle of stones. A
name on a map.
I read on a map a name whose Gaelic means
the Battlefield of the Big Men.
I think of yelling hosts, banners,
counterattacks, deployments. When I get there,
it's ten acres, ten small acres
of boggy ground.
I feel
I am looking through the same wrong end
of the same telescope
through which I look back through time
and see
Christ, Socrates, Dante — all the Big Men
picked out, on their few acres,
clear and tiny in
the misty landscape of history.

Up from that mist crowds
the present. This day has lain long,
has dozed late, till
the church bell jerks and, wagging madly
in its salty tower, sends its voice
clanking through the sabbath drowse.
And dark minds in black clothes gather like
bees to the hive, to share
the bitter honey of the Word, to submit
to the hard judgment of a God
my childhood God would have a difficulty
in recognising.
Ten yards from the sea's surge

they sing to Him beautiful praises
that surge like the sea,
in a bare stone box built
for the worship of the Creator
of all colours and between-colours, and of
all shapes, and of the holiness
of identity and of the purifying light-stream
of reason. The sound of that praise
escapes from the stone box
and takes its place in the ordinary communion
of all sounds, that are
Being expressing itself – as it does in its continuous,
its never-ending creation of leaves,
birds, waves, stone boxes – and beliefs,
the true and the false.

These shapes, these incarnations, have their own determined
identities, their own dark holiness, their
high absurdities. See how they make
a breadth and assemblage of animals,
a perpendicularity of creatures, from where,
three thousand feet up, two ravens go by
in their seedy, nonchalant way, down to
the burn-mouth where baby mussels
drink fresh water through their beards –
or down, down still, to where the masked conger eel
goes like a gangster through
the weedy slums at the sea's foot.

Greenshank, adder, wildcat, guillemot, seatrout,
fox and falcon – the list winds through
all the crooks and crannies of this landscape, all
the subtleties and shifts of its waters and
the prevarications of its air –
while roofs fall in, walls crumble, gables
die last of all, and man becomes,
in this most beautiful corner of the land,
one of the rare animals.

Up there, the scraping light
whittles the cloud edges till, like thin bone,

they're bright with their own opaque selves. Down here,
a skinny rosebush is an eccentric jug
of air. They make me,
somewhere between them,
a visiting eye,
an unrequited passion,
watching the tide glittering backward and making
its huge withdrawal from beaches
and kilted rocks. And the mind
behind the eye, within the passion,
remembers with certainty that the tide will return
and thinks, with hope, that the other ebb,
that sad withdrawal of people, may, too,
reverse itself and flood
the bays and the sheltered glens
with new generations replenishing the land
with its richest of riches and coming, at last,
into their own again.

Daft Dan

JOAN LINGARD

'Daft Dan's a silly old man, catch me, catch me, if you can!'

That was what the kids shouted after him, and then they ran, as he made a lunge towards them. But he wasn't as daft as they thought, oh no, not by a long way. Just because he didn't talk much and liked to take his time doing things. When he went down the street he'd stop and look, unlike all those people who went rushing past in their squealing cars, filling the air with nasty, smelly fumes, and he'd stroke the cats and dogs and smile at the little children who weren't big enough to shout after him, and he'd give them a sweetie out of his pocket. And he wasn't so old either, only fifty-eight, which Mrs Seddon from next door said wasn't old at all. She'd worked out his age for him on his last birthday and she'd made a cake and stuck eight blue candles into the chocolate icing, counting as she'd put them in, and he'd nodded his head, keeping time. She couldn't have put fifty-eight on, she explained; the cake wasn't big enough. When she'd lit the candles, her wee girl Helen had helped Dan blow them out and they'd all laughed. It had been a great birthday.

Dan lived by himself in the house where he'd been born, a house with a beautiful, bright, egg-yellow door. He had painted it himself. He had never slept a night in any other house but this. That was amazing, said Mrs Seddon; most people moved about a bit. Dan had lived there with his mother until two years ago, when she had died at the age of ninety. Dan kept her room the way she'd left it, he'd never even changed the sheets; he'd smoothed them out and pulled up the heavy crocheted cover and made the bed look nice. Every day he'd go into the room and touch her silver-backed brushes and mirror and the scent bottle that still smelt a bit of old faded roses when he put his nose to it and he'd sit in her chair by the window where the rays of sun filtered through the lace curtain, making the specks of dust dance in the air, and he'd have a chat with her. He talked more to his mother than to anyone else. Well, it was only natural, wasn't it?

'Mother,' he'd say, 'I'm going to prune the roses today,' or 'The strawberries are on the turn, we'll be picking them in a day or two.' And when they were ready he would pass a few over the fence to Mrs Seddon. He had a bit of everything in his garden: flowers, vegetables, fruit. 'Your garden's a right jungle, Dan,' Mrs Seddon said. 'A lovely jungle. It's just a riot of colour. A real riot.'

On the day that the first strawberries were ripe, he took three big ones in a bag and set off down the street, looking in at Mrs Seddon's to put a big red berry into Helen's little cupped hand. Like a flower it was. He ran his finger round the crease on her wrist. Mrs Seddon smiled and hugged Helen tightly to her and Dan smiled. He never called when Mr Seddon was in. He didn't like Mr Seddon. He was a big hard man, a man with heavy feet, a bad man; he beat his wife, who had eyes as blue as the delphiniums in Dan's border. Once he'd walked into their kitchen not knowing that Mr Seddon was home, just when he was lifting his hand to his wife and she was cowering against the wall, kind of slack looking, like a rag doll, with her arm up over her face. Dan had tried to catch hold of Mr Seddon's arm but he hadn't been a match for the younger man, who'd been in the pub and was in a terrible rage. Dan couldn't understand how a man with a wife like Mrs Seddon could be so angry. Mr Seddon had booted him out of the door and he'd gone sprawling face-down in their yard, and behind him, he could hear, coming from the house, the sound of a woman crying. He had thought his own throat was going to burst wide open.

'Stay away from my wife and child, d'you hear?' Mr Seddon had shouted before he slammed the door. After that, if he saw Dan as much as glancing over the garden fence, he'd say, 'What are you looking at?' and Dan would look away. Mrs Seddon said he wasn't such a bad man, her husband, not really, except when the drink took him. And he had never been the same since he'd lost his job. He went out every morning and he stayed away for the day. Spent it in pubs and snooker halls, she thought.

From the Seddons' Dan went to the Boyles'. They lived further down the street in a house with a bright blue door. Christopher was playing with a dump truck in the front garden. 'Vroom, vroom,' he was saying as he bumped the truck over the grass, his sturdy legs with their dimpled knees pushing it along. Dan held a strawberry out on the palm of his hand. Christopher jumped off the dump truck and came to collect it. Juice squirted out of his little round mouth as he stuffed the fruit in. He had lovely blond hair that Dan liked to touch. He did it gently, not ruffling the silky strands.

The Boyles' blue door opened and Christopher's mother looked out. 'Oh, it's you, Dan,' she said. 'You can't be too careful these days.'

Dan nodded, gave Christopher's head a final pat and crossed the road to the house whose door needed painting. It was a pity about the door, but this was the child he liked best, even better than Mrs Seddon's Helen, thiough he didn't like her mother as much as he did Mrs Seddon, not half as much.

Mary was four going on five, she had told Dan that herself. She loved to talk, like a bird chattering on a high wire. She had eyes as black as buttons and curly black hair that sprang from his fingers when he pulled it. He didn't really pull it, of course; he wouldn't hurt a single hair on her head.

'Mary! Come here at once!'

Mary's mother was on the doorstep, with her hip jutting out. Mrs Kelly was a sharp, angular woman; everything about her was sharp. Her voice, her nose, her chin, her elbows. Her eyes were like tacks. Jab, jab, jab, they went, piercing Dan. He flinched, drew back.

Mrs Kelly swooped down on her daughter, like a big black bird snatching its prey. 'How many times do I have to tell you!' she demanded, shaking the child so that Dan saw her bones rattle within the smooth envelope of her body. And the strawberry, the biggest from his garden, which he had put into her soft hand, shot from her grasp on to the pavement where it lay squashed and ruined. Mary set up a wail, soft and low, then brought up the pitch until it sounded like the singing noise Dan sometimes heard coming from his water pipes. He went home with the noise of it ringing in his ears.

Next morning, when he was working in his front garden, bent over his dahlias, tying them up, he heard Mrs Kelly's voice going past his hedge.

'He should be put away, Eileen, I'm telling you.'

'Sure he's harmless, Betty.' This voice belonged to Mrs Clarke, who had a lilac-coloured door at the bottom of the street. 'He just loves children. Our two think he's great.'

'But that's where the trouble comes, don't you see? It's often somebody they know . . .' The voices moved away with the wind.

Whispers. Buzz, buzz, buzz. Like wasps. Dan flapped his hands around his ears but the noise would not go away.

He went indoors to talk to his mother. 'I do love the children, Mother, but where's the harm in that? *Suffer the little children to come unto me.*' Hadn't his mother often read those words to him? She'd been a God-fearing woman who'd loved her Bible. He put his hand on the Book now. 'But you weren't that fond of Mrs Kelly, were you, Mother?' She had said there was something sleekit about Mrs Kelly and only God knew who the father of Mary was for there had never been a Mr Kelly on the scene. She had been sure that the Good Lord would see fit to punish her in his own time.

In the afternoon, as he sat at his window drinking tea from his Coronation mug, he saw Mary pass the gate with her granny. She was dancing at the end of her granny's hand. They were going to the zoo; Mary had told him a day or two ago. Her mother would have gone to the shops more than likely; she loved shopping, never passed up a chance to rake round the big stores downtown. She'd come home with spots of red in her cheeks and her hands full of bulging plastic bags with writing on the sides and her fast-moving heels going clickety-click on the pavement.

In the middle of Dan's table, amongst the pots and pans and dishes, were three especially big strawberries, even bigger than yesterday's harvest. They'd appeared this morning amongst the straw like a miracle. They were real beauties.

Carefully, lovingly, he placed the strawberries inside an old bakery bag and went out. The toes of his old fawn slippers led the way to Mary's house. Slap, slap, slap, they went, going out in front of him. The slippers were a bit frayed and Mrs Seddon had said it was time he was getting new ones. You can't throw old friends away, he had wanted to tell her, but he had just stood there shaking his head and he had thought she'd understood for she'd nodded and not said any more.

Mary's house looked quiet. He undid the latch and opened the gate and then tiptoed round the side, the way the children did when they were playing games. His slippers made no sound. In the garden Mary had a little house – a Wendy house it was called – and it was there that he would leave the strawberries and when she came back she'd think the fairies had left them. He'd set them out on the little doll's plates that she had.

He glanced first towards Mrs Kelly's house and saw that the back-room downstairs curtain was drawn, except for a vee in the middle. He could imagine Mrs Kelly's thin hands yanking the curtain across. He went up to the window and cupping his hands around his eyes, looked in. His nose bumped against the glass.

What he saw through the vee on the window made the blood rush to his head. There, lying on the floor in front of the unlit fire, were a man and a woman entwined together. Her legs were thin and witch-like; his back was thick and solid, like a bull's. Dan's head buzzed as if a swarm of wasps had found its way in.

Mrs Kelly and Mr Seddon lifted their heads to the side and saw him. They froze, like flies caught in jam. Their eyes bulged, like frogs' eyes.

'Fornication!' yelled Dan, dropping his three ripe strawberries. 'Fornication!' The big long word had come soaring into him as if from outer space and was winging round and round his head, like a trapped bird. It was a word from the Good Book, he knew that, He ran all the way up the street to his house, shouting it, then he shut his egg-yellow door and locked himself in.

It was the next day before they came for him. Round the edge of his mother's curtain he saw their fat pink fingers curling over the top of his gate and through the humming in his ears he heard the sound of their feet as they came up his garden path. Tramp, tramp, tramp. Busy-bodies in dark suits and Mrs Kelly following at their heels, yapping in her high sharp voice. 'Interfering', she was saying and 'touching'. 'Our Mary'll tell you.' Mr Seddon was talking, too. 'He couldn't keep his hands off our Helen.' Mrs Seddon was crying. 'He didn't mean any harm,' she was saying.

Not all there, he heard. A menace.

A dark arm shot out towards the side of his front door and the sound of the bell pierced his ears.

'It's for his own good,' said Mrs Kelly to Mrs Clarke as they passed Dan's gate. 'It's better that he's looked after, isn't it, by people who know what they're doing? I mean, he *wasn't* all there, was he?' And she twirled a long-nailed finger at her forehead. 'What can you do with people when they've got a slate loose? We've got to think of the kids, haven't we? God knows what he might have got up to!'

The weeds grew high in Dan's garden, choking the delphiniums and smothering the strawberry plants. Mr Seddon, glancing over the fence, swore and complained that it would do nothing for property values in the street.

The older kids chucked stones at the egg-yellow door and chanted, 'Daft Dan's a dirty old man, catch me, catch me, if you can!' And then they ran, since it had become a habit.

Las Vegas

EDWIN MORGAN

They crouch at handles day and night.
They crunch each mental fruit in sight.
They nurse their options through the blight.

The air-conditioning is cool.
Any found sweating is a fool,
and swearing is tales out of school.

Unstubbed cigarettes, worms of ash;
loosened tie and drooping tache;
dreams of streams of cash to stash.

What is it, moon, dawn, who cares?
Time shadows them unawares,
their teeth whistle threadbare airs.

Not hungry yet? They're thin with hope.
They glaze and twitch, but not from dope,
lay figures in an endless soap.

Outside, the sky is teatime blue.
The wet bikinis are see-through.
The pool has shrieks. Li-lo or do.

But inside, it is never late.
What you do is done by fate.
And light burns hard, inveterate.

Friendly Voices

DILYS ROSE

I have been here too long. The city has shrunk into a village. *Incestuous* is a word bandied about the place by the stretching web of people I know. Not that I have a wide circle of friends – I have never been especially liberal with my affections and intimacy is something for which I have always had a certain reserve. Incestuous is not an exact description but close enough. Unwholesome enough. Yet we are not people who wish to be associated with the dirty underside of life, the margins of existence, the underdog, subculture. We talk about it, of course; we are all too aware of our tenuous position and ambiguous relationship and sympathise with those who, through no fault of their own, have found themselves on the fraying edge of our society.

It's the dug. Feart for it. Doesny say, like, but Raj knows well enough. Raj can smell the fear on her. Dirty big bastard that he is, makes straight for the crotch, pokes his wet nose into her baggy jeans. Ah let him sniff about a bit until she starts to get panicky, then ah call him aff and slap his arse so the both of them know who's boss around here. But ah'm an animal lover, a big softy where Raj is concerned. Love me love ma dug.

We talk about it, about them, but keep our distance. We have created areas of safety for ourselves or at least put in speak-entry systems and requested unlisted telephone numbers from British Telecom. We take certain routes through the city, avoid others. We know well enough what those other routes are like. We've seen them all before; in our student days when everything was briefly, falsely equal and later, as young professionals, early in our careers when we preached and practised a hands-on approach. Grass roots. We got down to grass roots. Not that grass was a particularly common feature of the landscape.

Once Raj has settled at ma feet, the doctor crosses her legs and clutches

the top knee. Funny, never seen the wummin in a skirt. Probably a
policy no tae send them up here showing a leg, in case us lot, us *animals*
get funny. Funny peculiar but. No supposed tae come up here on her ain,
anyway, supposed tae have a mate wi her, for protection like. Ah tellt her
she should get a dug. Hours a fun and guaranteed tae keep trouble at bay.
That's unless trouble's got a dug of its ain.

There's no need to be reminded. It doesn't do any good to be reminded
of things we can't change. We're not heartless but practical, having
learned from experience that we can only function efficiently by
maintaining a certain distance. We have our own problems – who
doesn't – but we are, at heart, solvers, not sinkers.

When she comes in, she gies out this big sigh, like she's been holdin her
breath all the way up in the lift. Probably has because the lift stinks. No
all the time, no every single day. You might be lucky and catch it just
after it's been washed, in which case you just about choke on the dis-
infectant. Me, ah'm used tae it. Doesnae mean ah like it, but some things
you just put up wi.

   Anyway, after Raj has had his wee thrill, ah let her settle intae the
comfy chair and look around. She checks tae see how ah'm keeping the
place, see if she can find clues as tae how the medication's workin afore
she starts asking questions. No daft, this one, knows fine I'm a bloody
liar, knows I'll say the first thing that comes intae ma heid tae confuse
her. Tries tae get an idea of her ain, tae read between the fuckin lies ah
spin her.

   Shouldny come up here by hersel. Tryin tae make out she's brave and
that, but she's crappin it all the same. She's all edgy, hingin aff the chair
an that, eyes poppin out, kinda glaikit like, crossin the legs one way an
the other. Her jeans rub thegither at the crotch and the denim makes a
kinda scrapin sound. She gies a wee kid-on cough and pretends to be
dead interested in ma latest picture a Christ on the Cross. Crucified in a
field full a sheep. Quite pleased wi that one when ah done it but now
ah'm nae sure. Ah've got hunners a crucifixions anyway. She looks at ma
picture and ah look at her crotch. The dug has left a damp patch on her
jeans.

We've looked over the edge, know what lies there. We keep ourselves
under control, in check, watch out for the signs, of losing the place,
letting things slip. We know what to look out for. We're trained to spot
the signs, like the weatherman is trained to read the clouds. It's what we

do; spot the signs, make a forecast, though we like to think that the meanings are not fixed, that there are options involved, possibilities.

No ma type at all, very plain. Nae make-up, jewellery – bet she's got plenty jewellery but leaves it at hame in case somebody gies her a doin – cropped hair, wee tits – ah mean, no a lot going for her, tae ma mind. Money but, she'll have plenty a that, plenty dosh for putting hersel out for the likes a me. Nice car. Nifty wee two-seater. Seen it last time she came. Frae the windae. Pale blue convertible. Can just picture her on a sunny day – the sleeveless dress on, something loose and cool, the open-toed sandals – pulling down the hood and belting out tae Loch Lomond. Bet she's a fast driver. Bet she gets a buzz frae rammin the accelerator intae the flair. Wouldnae mind a whirl in her motor masel. All ah ever get's the fucking ambulance or, for a treat, the paddy wagon. Ah'm no complainin, but. Never say no tae a wee bit drama.

Of course, everything's relative. One only has to pick up the paper to be reminded just how much worse is daily life elsewhere: the Brazilian goldmine, say, where there is more malaria than gold; the bloody streets of Jerusalem or Johannesburg; the duplicitous back alleys of Bangkok or Rio, the hungry pavements of Bombay, New York, London. There are no goldmines on our doorstep, or war zones, no tin and board barrios, food queues. Yet.

She gets the chat goin so she can start tae suss out the state a the hoose. Sometimes ah clean up for her comin, sometimes ah dinnae. Depends. The place is a pure tip the day. Even if ah'm feeling no bad ah sometimes let the mess lie anyway, just tae see how she takes it. Like tae keep her on her toes. Dinnae want tae make her job too easy for her. Thinks she can tell the state a ma heid frae whether I've washed the dishes or no. And the chat's all geared tae pick up clues. Thinks she can earn her dosh by droppin in for tea and chitchat. Tries tae guess how ah'm daein frae what videos ah've watched, what magazines ah've read. Ah like it when she gets on tae that. Ah get a chance tae use ma imagination. Make up some brilliant titles, all horror and porn. Ah like tae get a wee blush goin on her, see that pulse start up at her throat. It's no a lot a response but she's no meant tae respond at all. It's her job tae stay neutral.

    She's no bad, but. Means well. Heart in the right place and all that guff. Wants tae help. Ah mean, she could've gone for one a they plum jobs in the private sector, analysin the rich and famous in some plush place down south. The nurse who comes tae gie me ma drugs, ma monthly jab, he tellt me she's top notch, expert in her field. Could've been rakin it in, sinkin the excess intae a second hame, somewhere aff the beaten track, far away frae the hurly-burly a Harley Street, or wherever they doctors hing about these days. But no, she's chosen tae make her livin frae the likes a me.

We complain, particularly about the larger issues, particularly on behalf of others. We are outraged by what is happening in the world, indeed the state of the globe is one of the most popular subjects for conversation amongst people like us. We lie awake at night and worry about the depletion of the ozone layer, preservatives in food, the destruction of the rain forest, the incidence of cancer near nuclear sites and the latest epidemics, about religious fundamentalism, neo-fascism, wars, riots, strikes, demonstrations, disasters natural and man-made – hurricanes, droughts and floods, about aphids, wild dogs and mad cows.

But we get up in the morning, the sun is shining, a scent of blossom is in the air, the grass is fresh and green beneath the litter and dog-shit we are growing accustomed to in the municipal parks. Under a clear sky, joggers, dogwalkers, cyclists, down-and-outs, students and parents of young children take the air together, at their own speeds. There are cycle lanes, walking lanes and jogging tracks. A bird sings. Blossom drifts in pink clouds above our heads. A man on a tractor cuts the grass and cleans up yesterday's mess. Another day passes without event, without people like us overstepping the boundary between the solvers and the sinkers. We have accumulated the life-skills required to keep our individual globes turning fairly smoothly. We stay clear of the edge but don't allow ourselves to forget what lies beyond it. We care. People like us care.

She's near drunk all her tea by the time she gets on tae the voices. Just about time for her tae get goin when she brings them up. Have they been friendly? she says. Eh? Your voices . . . she says. Aw aye. Have they been friendly? she says. Aye, ah says, nae bother. Ah'm gonnae tell her about the state a ma heid, when the singin starts up. Ma ears go that plugged-up way like when you've got headphones on and the singin loups round ma heid. It's that kinda auld folky stuff, nae many words you can make out, just a miserable kinda moany sound but sorta nice wi it, soothin like. The doctor's askin me somethin. Ah cannae hear what she's sayin, ah just know it's a question cos she's got her heid cocked tae the side, like a budgie. Raj is sittin at ma feet, lookin up at me wi big sad eyes, daft dug that he is. Sometimes ah think he hears ma voices tae. Ah give him a clap and tickle his belly. Loves a good tickle, so he does.

My office is bright, sunny. The walls are painted a pale, buttery yellow. On the wall facing the door is a small watercolour of a decorative plate and some pearly mussel shells. Behind my desk, above a shelf where I keep a constantly updated selection of leaflets (and my shade-loving ferns) is a calm abstract painting: *Contemplation 4*. There were three other remarkably similar paintings in the small gallery where I bought it. Any of them would have done just as well. Buying paintings is not a particular interest of mine. But I like those I have and they brighten up the office, give my patients (we call them clients) something to look at while they try to untangle their troubles, sort them into words, order the chaos of their minds into sensible phrases. People don't like to look you in the eye when they tell you their troubles.

It's no ma kind a singin but ah'm sittin here, hearin it, nae moving a muscle, an ah've got this amazin glow all over, ah'm feeling pure brilliant. Ah cannae explain it, ah've just got this kinda swellin in ma chest, like ma lungs is blowin up wi pure clean air, no the usual muck we suck in up this way. It's a gloomy auld tune, right enough, but it cheers me up no end. Here's this doctor, this consultant, sittin in ma chair, ma hoose, which may be a tip the day but isnae always. Next time she comes ah'm gonnae show her. I'll straighten it up, clean, aye well sometimes it doesnae seem worth the bother just for me and the dug.

Just like me she is, this doctor, on her ain. Naebody tae cuddle in the night. Least ah've got the dug if ah'm desperate. What's she got? What does she snuggle up tae on a cauld night? A hot water bottle, a teddy bear, a sex toy? Nae sae young neither tae be alane. Better get the skates on if she wants tae tie the knot. But then maybe she's one a they solitary types by choice, christ. Or queer, aye that's a possibility. Ah mean she's no what ah'd call a man's wummin.

Considering the design of the surgery, I'm fortunate to have a window. I've lined the sill with plants, the hardier varieties, those which require the minimum of attention. When I'm there, I play music, Vivaldi mostly, at low volume. I read somewhere about experiments on house plants to see how they responded to different kinds of music. Rock music made the plants wilt whereas Vivaldi made them flourish and wrap themselves lovingly around the sources of the music. I try to give a client the same opportunity to flourish. I listen, offer tea, an old but comfortable arm-chair, now and then a sympathetic nod. Mostly I listen until my client has told me the first version. It's usually a slow, tiresome process, for both of us. I ask a few more questions and the client redrafts the problem.

I try to give people an opportunity to flourish but don't claim a high level of success. The nature of the task being what it is and nothing being absolute, even an accurate assessment is rarely possible. My plants do better, when I'm around to tend them though. I'm rarely in the office these days. In the catchment area served by our practice, those who need me rarely come looking.

It's that singing. Ah just get this overpowerin . . . ah just get this feeling that she could really dae wi a big hug. Ah get tae ma feet, cross the room and lift her aff the chair. Ah'm staunin there, huggin her, fair away wi masel till ah see the look in her eyes and Jesus fuckin christ it's pure terror, the wummin's scared rigid, like a big cauld stane in ma hauns afore ah let go a her. And then the singing stops. Just like that. Like a tape being switched aff. Nae mair glow. That fuckin singin.

Doesny say anything about it, no a fuckin word. Just picks up her briefcase, tells me tae mind and be in for the nurse themorra, and goes. Raj chucks hissel at the door then slinks aff tae the kitchen. Needin fed but he'll have tae wait. Ah'm in nae mood for the fuckin dug. Ah hear her panicky wee steps as she hurries alang tae the lift. She'll no notice the stink on the way down, she'll be that happy just tae get the fuck out a here.

There she goes, marchin aff tae her motor, aff tae her next patient. Maybe she'll need a wee pit-stop somewhere, tae pull hersel thegither, get hersel nice and neutral again. When she's through wi us lot, put in her time, done her bit, she's gonnae nip back tae the surgery, tae her cheery wee office, take out ma file and bang in a new prescription. She's gonnae up the dosage, up it enough tae take away ma voices allthegither, blot them out, kill them aff. Didnae mean her any harm for fuck's sake. Christ, ah was tryin tae be nice but she'll no see it that way, will she? She'll see it as a fuckin problem, and up the dosage. Tae bring me back tae ma senses, back tae The Real World. Tae this. The morra. Jab day themorra. Ah get the feelin ma voices areny gonnae be fuckin friendly the night.

Homeless

JANET PAISLEY

skylight
           is bluebright gaps
skydark   starsparked
spaces in black
                    nightfaces
the pale ghost
                    of dawnmist
as the chillfist
                    of daybreaks
                        on bone
aches in her spine
            never rains but it pours
boardscreak
                    into floorspeech
the windreeks
            a morning stench
of garbage
            drenches
                    her senses
and daygears up
                    the street
in a crunch of trucks
                    she wakes
outside everydoor
                        inside
every mind   a closedsign
finds gettingup
                    is comingdown
and the ground
                    is always hard

Houses and Small Labour Parties

ALASDAIR GRAY

Eight men dug a trench beside a muddy crossroads, and the mud made two of the gang remember Italy, where they had fought in a recent war. These two had not known each other in Italy, but both remembered a dead German who lay at a crossroads near Naples, though one thought it was perhaps nearer Pisa. They discussed the matter when the gang paused for a smoke.

'Not Pisa, no, Pisa was miles away,' said one, 'Naples was the place. He was a handsome big fella at first. We used to call him Siegfried.'

'Our lot called him Adolf, because of the fuckin moustache,' said the other. 'He wasnae handsome for fuckin long.'

'I don't remember a moustache, but you're right, he wasnae handsome for long. He went all white and puffy and swole up like a balloon – I think only his uniform stopped him bursting. The heavy traffic must have kept the rats away. Every time we went that road I hoped to God someone had shifted him but no, there he always was, more horrible than ever. Because eventually a truck ran over him and burst him up properly. Do you mind that?'

'I mind it fuckin fine.'

'Every time we went that road we would say, "I wonder how old Siegfried's doing", and look out for him, and there was always something to see, though at last it was only the bones of a foot or a bit of rag with a button on it.'

There was a silence. The older navvies thought about death and the youngest about a motorcycle he wanted to buy. He was known for being the youngest of them and fond of motorcycles. Everybody in the gang was known for something. Mick the ganger was known for saying queer things in a solemn voice. One navvy was known for being a Highlander, one for having a hangover every morning, one for being newly married. One of the ex-army men was known for his war stories, the other for his sexual adjectives. One of them was a communist who thought *The Ragged*

Trousered Philanthropists better than the Bible and kept trying to lend it;
but schooling had given most of them a disgust of books. Only Old Joe
looked into the book and he said it was a bit out of date. The communist
wanted to argue the point but Old Joe was known for being silent as well
as old. The youngest navvy liked working with these folk, though he
hardly ever listened to what they said. Too many of them wanted his
attention. They remembered, or thought they remembered, when they
too had been just out of school, sixteen and good-looking, happy because
their developing muscles could still enjoy the strain of working overtime,
happy because it was great to earn a wage as big as their fathers earned.
The worst-paid workers reach the peak of the earning power early in life.

'The signoras!' announced the story-teller suddenly, 'the signorinas!
They were something else. Am I right? Am I wrong?'

'Aye, the fuckin signoras were somethin fuckin else,' said the other
ex-army man. With both hands he shaped a huge bosom on the air
before his chest.

'I'll give you a bit of advice, Ian,' the story-teller told the youngest
navvy. 'If you ever go to Italy take a few tins of bully beef in your
suitcase. There is *nothing*, I'm telling you, *nothing* you won't get from the
Italian signorinas in return for a can of bully beef.'

'That advice may be slightly out of date,' said Mick the ganger.

'You're sticking up for the Tally women because they're Papes and so
are you, ye fuckin Fenian Irish Papal prick ye,' said one of the ex-army
men pleasantly.

'He's right, of course,' the ganger told the youngest navvy, 'I am a
Papal Fenian. But if these warriors ever return to Italy they may find the
ladies less welcoming now the babies have stopped starving.' He nipped
his cigarette, stuck it under his cap brim above the right ear and lifted his
pick. The gang began digging again.

Though their work was defined as 'unskilled' by the Department of
Labour they worked skilfully in couples, one breaking the ground with a
pick, the other shovelling loose earth and stones from under his partner's
feet and flinging it clear of the ditch. At the front end Mick the ganger
set a steady pace for all of them. The youngest navvy was inclined to go
too fast, so Mick had paired him with Old Joe who was nearly sixty, but
remained a good workman by pacing himself very carefully. The two ex-
army men were liable to slow down if paired with each other, so Mick
always paired one of them with himself. The gang belonged to a work-
force of labourers, brickies, joiners, plumbers, slaters, electricians,
painters, drivers, foremen and site clerks who were enlarging a city by
turning a hillside into a housing estate. During the recent war (which had

ended twelve years before but still seemed recent to all who remembered it) the government had promised there would be no return to unemployment afterwards, and every family would eventually have a house with a lavatory and bath inside. The nation's taxes were now being spent on houses as well as armed forces, motorways, public health et cetera, so public housing was now profitable. Bankers and brokers put money into firms making homes for the class of folk who laboured to build them. To make these fast and cheaply, standards of spaciousness and craftsmanship were lowered and makeshifts used which had been developed during the war. Concrete replaced stonework. Doors were light wooden frames with a hardboard sheet nailed to each side. Inner walls were frames surfaced with plasterboard that dented if a door-knob swung hard against it. A tall man could press his fingers to the ceilings without standing on tiptoe. But every house had a hot-water system, a bath and flush lavatory, and nearly everyone was employed. There was so much work that firms advertised for workers overseas and natives of the kingdom were paid extra to work at weekends and during public holidays. In the building industry the lowest paid were proudest of what they earned by overtime work so most of this gang worked a six-day week. A labourer who refused overtime was not exactly scorned as a weakling, but thought a poor specimen of his calling. Recently married men were notoriously poor specimens, but seldom for more than a fortnight.

A heavily built man called McIvor approached the trench and stood for a while watching the gang with a dour, slightly menacing stare which was a tool of his trade. When his presence was noticed by the ganger, McIvor beckoned him by jerking his head a fraction to the side. Mick laid his pick carefully down, dried his sweating face with a handkerchief, muttered, 'No slacking, men, while I confabulate with our commanding officer,' and climbed out of the trench. He did not confabulate. He listened to McIvor, stroked his chin then shouted, 'Ian! Over here a minute!'

The youngest navvy, surprised, dropped his spade, leapt from the trench and hurried to them. McIvor said to him, 'Do you want some overtime? Sunday afternoons, one to five.'

'Sure.'

'It's gardening work but not skilled – weeding, cutting grass, that sort of thing. It's at the house of Mr Stoddart, the boss. He'll give the orders. The rate is the usual double time. You get the money in your weekly pay packet.'

'I thought Old Joe did that job.'

'He does, but the boss says Joe needs help now. Yes or no?'

'Aye. Sure,' said the youngest navvy.

'Then I'll give you a word of advice. Mick here has pointed you out as a good worker so you'd better be, because the boss has a sharp eye for slackers and comes down on them like a ton of bricks. He also has a long memory, and a long arm. If you don't do right by Mr Stoddart you won't just get yourself in the shit, you'll make trouble for Mick here who recommended you. Right, Mick?'

'Don't put the fear of death into the boy,' said the ganger. 'Ian will do fine.'

In the bothy where the navvies had their lunch one of the ex-army men said loudly in his cheeriest voice, 'I see the fuckin Catholics are sticking to-fuckin-gether as per fuckin usual.'

'Could that be a hostile remark?' the ganger asked Ian. 'Do you think the foul-mouthed warrior is talking about us?'

'Fuckin right I'm talking about yous! You could have gave the fuckin job to a fuckin family-man like me with fuckin weans to feed but no, you give it to a fuckin co-religionist who's a fuckin wean himself.'

'I'm not a Catholic!' said the youngest navvy, astonished.

'Well how do you come to be so fuckin thick with Mick the Papal prick here?'

'I recommended the infant of the gang for three reasons,' said the ganger, 'One, he is a bloody hard worker who gets on well with Old Joe. Two, some family-men enjoy Sunday at home. Three, if one of us start working around the boss's house he'll get the name of being a boss's man, which is good for nobody's social life, but Ian is too young to be thought that, just as Joe is too old.'

'Blethers!' said the communist, 'You are the boss's man here, like every ganger. You're no as bad as bastarding McIvor, but he comes to you for advice.'

'Jesus, Mary and Joseph!' cried Mick to the youngest navvy, 'for the love of God get out of this and apprentice yourself to a decent trade! Go up to the joiners' bothy and talk to Cameron – they're wanting apprentice joiners.'

'I'm not a Catholic, I've *never* been a Catholic,' said the youngest navvy, looking around the others in the bothy with a hurt, alarmed and pleading expression. The Highlander (who was also suspected of being Catholic because he came from Barra, and someone had said everyone from that island were Catholics) said, 'You are absolved – go in peace,' which caused general amusement.

'Did you hear me, Ian?' said the ganger sharply, 'I told you to get out of this into a decent trade.'

'I might, when I've bought my Honda,' said the youngest navvy thoughtfully. He saw the sense in the ganger's advice. A time-served tradesman was better paid and had more choices of work than a labourer, but during the apprentice years the wage would be a lot less.

'Why did a clever fella like you never serve your time as a tradesman, Mick?' asked the communist.

'Because at sixteen I was a fool, like every one of us here, especially that silly infant. I never wanted a motorbike, I wanted a woman. So here I am, ten years later, at the peak of my profession. I've a wife and five children and a job paying me a bit more than the rest of you in return for taking a lot of lip from a foul-mouthed warrior and from a worshipper of Holy Joe Stalin.'

'You havenae reached the peak yet, Mick,' said the communist. 'In a year or three they'll give you McIvor's job.'

'No, I'll never be a foreman,' said Mick sombrely. 'The wages would be welcome, but not the loneliness. Our dirty-tongued Orange friend will get that job – he enjoys being socially obnoxious.'

The foreman had given the youngest navvy a slip of paper on which was written *89 Balmoral Road, Pollokshields*, and the route of a bus that would take him past there, and the heavily underlined words *1p.m. on the dot.* The boy's ignorance of the district got him to the boss's house seven minutes late and gasping for breath. He lived with his parents on a busy thoroughfare between tenements whose numbers ran into thousands. When the bus entered Balmoral Road he saw number 3 on a pillar by a gate and leapt off at the next stop, sure that 89 must be nearby. He was wrong. After walking fast for what seemed ten minutes he passed another bus stop opposite a gate pillar numbered 43, and broke into a jog-trot. The sidewalk was a gravel path with stone kerb instead of a pavement, the road was as wide as the one where he lived, but seemed wider because of the great gardens on each side. Some had lawns with flower-beds behind hedges, some shrubberies and trees behind high walls, and both sorts of driveways leading up to houses which seemed as big as castles. All of well-cut stone, several imitated castles by having turrets, towers and oriel windows crowned with battlements. Signboards at two or three entrances indicated nursing homes, but names carved on gate pillars ('Beech Grove', 'Trafalgar', 'Victoria Lodge') suggested most houses were private, and so did curtains and so did ornaments in the windows. Yet all had several rooms big enough to hold the complete two-room flat where he lived with his parents, or one of the three-room-and-kitchen flats being built on the site where he laboured. But the

queerest thing about this district was the absence of people. After the
back of the bus dwindled to an orange speck in the distance, then
vanished, the only moving things he saw were a few birds in the sky and
what must have been a cat crossing the road a quarter-mile ahead. His
brain was baffled by no sight or sign of buildings he thought always went
with houses: shops, a post office, school or church. Down the long length
of the road he could not even see a parked car or telephone box. The
place was a desert. How could people live here? Where did they buy
their food and meet each other? Seeing number 75 on another gate pillar
he broke into an almost panic-stricken run.

Number 89 was not the biggest house he had seen but still impressive.
On rising ground at a corner, it was called 'The Gables' and had a lot of
them. The front garden was terraced with bright beds of rose bushes
which must have been recently tended by a professional gardener. A low,
new brick wall in front hid none of this. The young navvy hurried up a
drive of clean granite chips which scrunched so loudly underfoot that he
wanted to walk on the trim grass verge, but feared his boots would dent
it. Fearful of the wide white steps up to the large front door he went
crunching round the side to find a more inviting entrance, and discovered
Old Joe building a rockery in the angle of two gables.

'Hullo, Joe. Am I late? Is he angry?'

'I'm your gaffer today so don't worry. Fetch ower yon barrow and
follow me.'

Behind the house was a kitchen garden, a rhododendron shrubbery
and a muddy entry from a back lane. Near the entry lay a pile of small
boulders and a mound of earth with a spade in it. Joe said, 'Bring me a
load of the rocks then a load of the earth and keep going till I tell ye
different. And while we're away from the house I don't mind telling you
ye're on probation.'

'What's that supposed to mean?'

'He watches us. He's seen you already.'

'How? Why do ye think that?'

'You'll know why when he talks to ye later.'

As they worked on the rockery the young navvy looked cautiously
about and gradually grew sure they were the only folk in the garden. The
walls of the house where they worked were blank, apart from a wee
high-up window that probably ventilated a lavatory. When he wheeled
the barrow to the back entry he was in view of larger windows. He kept
bringing boulders and earth to Joe who worked kneeling and sometimes
said, 'Put that there, son', or 'Give a shovelful here'.

Nearly an hour passed then Joe sighed, stood slowly up, straightened his shoulders and said, 'Five minutes.'

'I'll just get another load,' said the young navvy, lifting the shafts of the barrow. He was uneasily aware of the black little lavatory window above and behind him.

'We're entitled to five-minute spells,' said Old Joe quietly. 'We need them.'

'I don't need them. And I was late, you werenae.'

He went off with the barrow, loaded it and found Joe working when he returned. An hour later a gaunt, smartly dressed lady looked round a corner, called 'Your tea is in the tool-shed,' then vanished behind the corner.

'Was that his wife?' asked the young navvy.

'His housekeeper. Are you working through the tea-break too?'

The young navvy blushed.

The tool-shed, like the garage, was part of a big newly built outhouse. It was windowless, and had a roller shutter door facing the back entry. It smelt of cement, timber and petrol; had shelves and racks of every modern gardening and construction tool, all shiningly new; also a workbench with two mugs of tea and a plate of chocolate biscuits on it; also a motorcycle leaning negligently against a wall, though there were blocks for standing it upright.

'A Honda!' whispered the young navvy, going straight to it and hunkering down so that his eyes were less than a foot from the surface of the thing he worshipped, 'Who's is this?'

'The boss's son's.'

'But he hasnae been using it,' said the young navvy indignantly, noting the flat tyres, dust on seat and metal, dust on a footpump and kit of keys and spanners strewn near the front wheel. What should be shining chromium was dull, with rust spots.

'He's got better things to think of,' said Joe after swallowing a mouthful of tea. 'He's a student at the Uni.'

'Why does he no sell it?'

'Sentimental reasons. His da gave it him as a present, and he doesnae need the money.'

The young navvy puffed out his cheeks and blew to convey astonishment, then went over to the bench. Since they were not in sight or earshot of anyone he said, 'What's the boss like?'

'Bossy.'

'Come on, Joe! There's good and bad bosses. What sort is he?'

'Middling to average. You'll soon see.'

Ten minutes later they returned to the garden and worked for over an hour before Joe said, 'Five minutes,' and straightened his back, and surveyed his work with a critical eye. The young navvy paused and looked too. He could see the rocks were well balanced and not likely to sink under heavy rains, but the impending presence of the unseen Stoddart (maybe the biggest and bossiest boss he would ever meet) made him restless. After a minute he said, 'I'll just get us another load,' and went off with the barrow.

Half an hour later the rockery was complete. As they stood looking at it the young navvy suddenly noticed there were three of them and for a moment felt he had met the third man before. He was a massive man with a watchful, impassive face, clean white open-necked shirt, finely creased flannel slacks and white canvas sports shoes. At last the stranger, still looking at the rockery, said, 'Seven minutes late, Why?'

'I got off at the wrong stop — I didnae know the street was so long.'

'That makes sense. What's your name, youngster?'

'Ian Maxwell.'

'Apart from the lateness (which will *not* be docked from your wages) you've done well today, Ian. You too, Joe. A very decent rockery. The gardener can start planting tomorrow. But the day's work is not yet done as Joe knows, but perhaps as you do *not* know, Ian. Because now the barrow, spade, fork, trowel go back to the tool-shed and are *cleaned* – cleaned thoroughly. There's a drain in the floor and a wall-tap with a hose attached. Use them! I don't want to find *any* wee crumbs of dirt between the tyre and the hub of that barrow. A neglected tool is a wasted tool. What you'd better know from the start, Ian (if you and me are going to get on together) is that I am not gentry. I'm from the same folk you are from, so I know what you are liable to do and not do. But do right by me and I'll do right by you. Understood?'

The young navvy stared, hypnotised by the dour impassive face now turned to him. Suddenly it changed. The eyes stayed watchful but the mouth widened into what the young navvy supposed was a smile, so he nodded. The big man patted him on the shoulder and walked away.

The navvies went to the tool-shed and cleaned the tools in silence. The younger was depressed, though he did not know why. When they had returned the tools to their places (which were easy to see, because there were three of everything so a gap in the ranks was as obvious as a missing tooth) the young navvy said, 'Do we just leave now?'

'No. We wait for the inspection.'

They did not wait long. There was a rattling of at least two locks then an inner door opened and Stoddart came through carrying a tray with two glasses, a whisky bottle and a jug of water. His inspection was a quick sideways glance towards the tool-racks before he said, 'How old are you, Ian?'

'Nearly seventeen.'

'Too young for whisky. I'm not going to teach you bad habits. But Joe and me haven't had our ne'erday yet. A bad thing, me forgetting old customs. A large one, Joe? Macallan's Glenlivet Malt?'

'Thanks, aye.'

'Water?'

'No thanks.'

'Quite right, better without . . . Good stuff, Joe?'

'Aye.'

'How's the old back, the old lumbago, Joe?'

'No bad, considering.'

'Aye, but age gets us all in the end – even me. I'm not as young as I was. We have to learn to take things easy, Joe.'

'Aye,' said Joe, and emptied the glass straight down his throat.

'God, that went fast!' said Stoddart. 'Another one, Joe?'

'Goodnight,' said Joe, and walked out.

'Goodnight Joe, and goodnight to you, Ian. See you next week on the dot of one, youngster. Joe will be taking a bit of a rest. Right?'

'Thanks,' said the young navvy, and hurried after Joe wondering why he had said 'thanks' instead of 'goodnight' when he had been given nothing, had not even been paid yet for his labour.

The young navvy overtook Joe walking into the back lane and said, 'Are you no going for a bus, Joe?'

'No. This is a shortcut.'

'Can I come with you?' asked the young navvy, wondering why he was asking. Joe said nothing. They walked beside each other in a lane with a brick wall on one side, a railway embankment on the other. It could have been in the depths of the country. Grass, daisies and clover grew between two parallel paths made by car wheels and the verges were thick with dandelions, dockens, thistles, burdock. Branches from trees in the gardens behind the wall hung overhead, and from the embankment hawthorns and brambles stuck thorny, leafy shoots between the sagging wires of the fence. The old and young navvy walked side by side in silence, each on one of the parallel tracks. The young one felt Joe was angry, feared it had to do with him, tried to think of something to say. And at last said, 'When the boss turned up beside us back there I thought he was McIvor at first.'

Joe said nothing.

'Don't *you* think he's a bit like McIvor, Joe?'

'Of course he's like McIvor. McIvor is a foreman. Stoddart is the foreman's foreman – the gaffer's gaffer. Of course he's like McIvor.'

'But he's cheerier than McIvor – he calls ye by your first name. Have you had drinks with him before, Joe?'

'That was the first and last.'

'The last. Why the last?'

'Because you've done for me.'

'What do you mean?' asked the young navvy, suddenly seeing exactly what the old one meant but confused by two amazements: amazement that the boss preferred him to Joe, amazement at the unfairness and speed of the result. Together these amazements stopped him feeling very happy or very angry. But he liked Joe so felt obliged to refer to the unfairness. 'Are you *sure* he doesnae ever want ye back, Joe? I never heard him say so.'

'Then you need your ears washed.'

'But that cannae be right, Joe! I've got more muscle than you but I havenae the head yet – the skill. That's why Mick keeps pairing us. If I'm working just by myself I won't do so much because I'll need to keep stopping to think.'

'Too true!' said Joe, 'Stoddart is stupider than he knows, but he's a boss so nobody can put him right. In a week or two when he sees you arenae doing as well as you did today he'll think you've started slacking so give you the heave and get in someone else. Or maybe no! If ye arrive ten minutes early every day, and work your guts out till he tells ye to stop, and if you take a five-minute tea-break or none at all when the housekeeper forgets ye – well, if ye sweat enough at showing you're a boss's man he'll maybe keep ye.'

Joe climbed over the fence and went up the embankment by a path slanting through willow herb. The young navvy followed, his confused feelings tinged by distress. Joe led him across three sets of railway lines to a gap in a fence of upright railway sleepers. They were now in a broad, unpeopled street between old warehouses.

'What should I do, Joe?' asked the young navvy. He was not answered, so said it again. After a long silence Joe suddenly said, 'Get out of this into civil engineering, son. No bastard can own you in civil engineering because ye travel all over. Highland power stations, motorways in the Midlands, reservoirs in Wales – if ye tire of one job ye just collect your jotters and wages, clear out the same day and go to another. Naebody minds. No questions asked. And the money, the overtime is phenomenal. Once at Loch Sloy I worked a forty-eight-hour stint – forty-eight hours with the usual breaks, of course, but I was on the job the whole time without one wink of sleep. Someone bet me I couldnae but I could and I did. Civil engineering is the life, son, for folk like you and me. Of course, most of the money goes on booze and betting, there's nothing much else to do with it. Some keep a wife and weans on the money but why bother? Ye only get to see them one week in six maybe. Family life is a con, a bloody imposition. Not that I'm advocating prostitutes! Keep clear of all women, son, is my advice to you: if they don't give you weans they'll give you some other disease. Chuck Stoddart and go into civil engineering. It's the only life for a man while he has his strength. That's what I did and I've never regretted it.'

Joe seldom said more than one sentence at a time so the young navvy brooded over this speech. Booze, betting and prostitutes did not attract him. He wanted to hurl himself through the air toward any target he chose, going faster than a mile a minute with maybe a girl clinging on a pillion behind. But a good bike cost nearly four hundred pounds. After paying his people two-thirds of his weekly earnings in return for the home and services he had enjoyed since infancy, about four pounds remained which (despite his intentions of saving three pounds a week) seemed always to get eaten up by tram, café, cinema, dancehall, football, haircut and clothes expenses – he had begun to like dressing well on his few nights out. But if he worked on a big civil engineering job in the Highlands, and did all the twelve or sixteen-hour shifts his strength allowed, and slept and ate cheaply in a workers' hostel, and paid his people a few shillings a week till he felt like returning, he might earn enough to buy a good bike in less than a year. Then the neglected Honda in the boss's tool-shed came to mind, and Stoddart's words 'A neglected tool is a wasted tool'. He decided that next Sunday, perhaps during the tea-break, he would set the Honda in its blocks, clean it and tidy away the tools. Stoddart would certainly notice this and say something during the five o'clock inspection, and the young navvy had a feeling this might lead to something useful. He did not know what, but found the prospect oddly exciting, though he still felt sorry for Joe.

While he pondered these things they crossed a bridge over a railway cutting and came to Kilmarnock Road. It was a busy road with the railway on one side and on the other wee shops and pubs on the ground floor of ordinary tenements. The young navvy knew this road well. He travelled it by tramcar six days a week from his home to the building site and back. He was perplexed to find it so near the foreign, almost secret city of huge rich houses. A few blocks away he noticed a sign of a station where a subway train would take him home in time for the usual family tea. His distress vanished. He said, 'I don't think my ma or da would like me going off to civil engineering just yet, Joe, but I'll take a crack at it one day. Thanks for the tip. See you the morrow.'

Joe nodded and they separated.

Shivering

IAIN CRICHTON SMITH

'Home is the place
where if you go to
they have to take you in.'

The sky takes us in,
the snow,
the streets without mercy.

I lie looking at the stars
shivering
as the stars are shivering.

The whole universe is shivering,
that magnificent jewellery
which I had once ignored.

Everything is shivering.
My teeth chatter
and I have nothing to say.

If this should happen
the state should shiver
and those who go past in furs.

To bed in the open!
O you with electric blankets
listen.

O you who switch off your light
as you mark the page
of your latest volume.

Remember that in tune with the stars
some are shivering.

In the winter's terrible indifference
as the snow falls lightly down,

and the wind from the east blows,
draughty,
in a place without doors.

Remember us, the cold ones,
whom the stars look down on
in windy complicity,

the jewellery of the rich,
distant, beautiful,

high above the unshaven faces.

A Mother Worries

LIZ LOCHHEAD

From the moment the Little White Bundle is stuck in your arms
And you're terrified in case you drop it, or it stops breathing,
And, whether its three hundred decibel howls mean a terminal tumour
Or else it's 'only teething' . . .
Or else it's the Croup, the Colic, the Beads it just swallowed or double
    pneumoniacutependicitis . . .
(And then when they're older, a mother tends to worry about
what the reason for the Ominous Quiet is)
But let's face it, in this infectious old world
Itching with Lassa Fever, diphtheria, smallpox, meningitis, teenage
    pregnancy, gonorrhoea and infantile paralysis.
While all a mother's got is a bottle of Dettol in the final analysis.
Well . . . A Mother Worries.

A mother knows she shouldn't try and keep them tied to the apron
    strings because they're bound to flee the coop
And the best a mother can hope for is that they'll occasionally pop home
    for the odd loan of ten quid or bowl of chicken soup,
But A Mother Worries.

A mother does her level best to warn them about the ever present
    dangers
Of alcoholism and sex and dope and taking sweets from strangers
But it's all water off a duck's back
As well to save your breath
Consideration of a Parent's Wishes
Is a fate worse than death –
Try and instil a sense of what's right
And still they treat this house like a hotel –
Day in day out, morning noon and night.

Well a mother doesn't want to nag or harp on, or use clichés or run the
     risk of sounding shrewish
But a mother whatever her colour and creed is fundamentally Jewish –
She worries!

Street-Sweeper

JAMES KELMAN

The sky was at the blueyblack pre-heavygrey stage of the morning and the gaffer was somewhere around. This is one bastard that was always around; he was always hiding. But he was somewhere close right now and Peter could sense his presence and he paused. It wasnt a footstep but he turned to see over his shoulder anyway, walked a few more paces then quickly sidled into a shop doorway, holding the brush vertical, making sure the top of his book wasnt showing out his pocket. This was no longer fun. At one time in his life it mightve been but no now, fuck, it was just bloody silly. And it wisni funny. It just wisni fucking funny at all. These things were beginning to happen to him more and more and he was still having to cope. What else was there. In this life you get presented with your choices and that's that, if you canni choose the right ones you choose the wrong ones and you get fucked some of the time; most of the time some people would say. He closed his eyes, rubbed at his brow, smoothing the hair of his eyebrows. What was he to do now, he couldni make it back to the place he was supposed to be at, no without being spotted. Aw god. But it gave him a nice sense of liberty as well, it was an elation, quite fucking heady. Although he would have to move, he would – how long can you stay in a doorway! Hey, there was a big cat watching him, it was crouched in beside a motor-car wheel. Ha, christ. Peter chuckled. He was seen by a cat your honour. There he was in a doorway, having skived off because he had heard about a forced entry to a newsagent shop and thought there mightve been some goods lying available to pilfer.

Objection!

Overruled.

Ah but he was sick of getting watched. He was. He was fucking sick of it. The council have a store of detectives. They get sent out spying on the employees, the workers lad the workers, they get sent out spying on them. Surely not. The witness has already shown this clearly to be the case your Honour. Has he indeed. Aye, fuck, he has, on fucking numerous occasions, that's how come he got the boys out on strike last March.

Ah.

Naw but he's fucking sick of it, he really is. High time he was an adult. Here he is forty-seven years of age and he's a boy, a wee lad – in fact, he is all set to start wearing short trousers and ankle-socks and a pair of fast-running sandshoes (plimsolls for the non-Scottish reader). What was he to do but that is the problem, that is the thing you get faced with all the bloody time, wasnt it just bloody enervating. But you've got your brush you've got your brush and he stepped out and was moving, dragging his feet on fast, dragging because his left leg was a nuisance, due to a fucking disability that made him limp – well it didni *make* him limp, he decided to limp, it was his decision, he could have found some new manner of leg-motoring which would have allowed him not to limp, by some sort of circumlocutory means he could have performed a three-way shuffle to offset or otherwise bypass the limp and thus be of normal perambulatory gait. This was these fucking books he read. Peter was a fucking avid reader and he had got stuck in the early Victorian era, even earlier, bastards like Goldsmith for some reason, that's what he read. Charles fucking Lamb, that's who he read; all these tory essayists of the pre-chartist days, that other bastard that didni like Keats. Why did he read such shite. Who knows, they fucking wreaked havoc with the syntax, never mind the fucking so-called sinecure of a job, the street cleaning. Order Order. Sorry Mister Speaker. But for christ sake, for christ sake.

Yet you had to laugh at his spirit I mean god almighty he was a spirited chappie, he was, he really and truly was. But he had to go fast. There was danger ahead. No time for quiet grins. Alright he was good, he was still doing the business at forty-seven, but no self-congratulatory posturing if you please, even though he might still be doing it, even though he was still going strong at the extraordinarily advanced age of thrice fifteen-and-two-thirds your honour, in the face of extraordinarily calamitous potentialities to wit said so-called sinecure. Mister Speaker Mister Speaker, this side of the House would request that you advise us as to the appertaining set of circumstances of the aforementioned place and primary purpose of said chappie's sinecure so-called. Uproar. A Springburn street. Put on the Member for Glasgow North. The Member for Glasgow North has fuckt off for a glass of claret. Well return him post-haste.

But the goodwife. Has the goodwife a word to say. Yes, indeed. The goodwife would bat him one on the gob. She thought all this was dead and buried. She thought the sinecure was not deserving of the 'so-called' prefixed reference one iota, i.e. sinecure *qua* sinecure in the good lady's opinion.

She wouldni think it was possible but, it's true, she thought it was all over as far as the problematics were concerned. Pussycats pussycats, I tought I saw. But there you are, getting to the doddering stage, being spotted by a crouching cat, so much for his ability to cope, to withstand the helter skelter, the pell mell, the guys in the darkblue and the bulky shoulders. Bejasus he was getting fucking drunk on the possibility of freedom, a genuine liberty, one that would be his prior to deceasement. What he fancied was a wee periscope from the coffin, so he could just lie there watching the occasional passersby, the occasional birdie or fieldmouse:

he was into another doorway and standing with his back pressed into the wall, his eyes shut tight, but lips parted, getting breath, listening with the utmost concentration. Nothing. Nothing o christ why was he an atheist this of all times he felt like screaming a howsyrfather yr paternoster a quick hail mary yr king billy for christ sake what was it was it a fucking footfall he felt like bellowing, bellowing the fucking place down, it would show them it would show them it would display it, it would display how he was and how he could bellow his laughter in the face of the fucking hidebound universe of them, fucking moribund bastirts – was it the gaffer? He pulled the brush in, held it like an upright musket of the old imperialist guard, India or Africa yr Lordship.

Carol thought it was all dead and buried. She did, she truly truly did. His eyes were shut and his lips now closed, the nostrils serving the air channels or pipes, listening with the utmost concatenation of the earular orifices. Not to scream. Not to make a sound. Another minute and he would go, he would move, move off, into the greying dawn.

He was safe now for another few minutes. It was over, a respite o lord how brief is this tiny candle flicker. Peasie Peasie Peasie. For this was his nickname, the handle awarded him by the mates, the compañeros, the compatriots, the comrades: Peasie.

It didni even matter the profit but this was the fucking thing! Maybe he got there and the newsagent turned out to be a grocer for god sake how many cartons of biscuits can you plank out in some backcourt! Fucking radio rental yr Lordship, Mind you the profit was of nae account, nane at all. Neither the benefits thereon. If there were benefits he didni ken what they were. He shook his head. Aright, aright me boy, me lad. There was a poor fucker lying on the grun ahead. There was. Peter approached cautiously. It was a bad sign. It was. If the security forces martialled, and they would, then they would be onto him in a matter of hours, a couple of hours, maybe even one; he would need a tale to tell. Diarrhoea. Diarrhoea, the saviour of the working classes. He had to go to the loo and spend some several minutes, maybe thirty, unable to leave in case the belly ructured yet again. But the body was a bad sign. Poor bastard.

Peter knelt by the guy. He was still alive, his forehead warm and the tick at the temple, a faint pulsing. But should he drag him into a close-mouth No, of course not, plus best to leave him or else

but the guy was on his back and that was not good. Peter laid down his brush and did the life-saving twist, he placed the man's right arm over his left side, then raised and placed his right leg also over his left side, then gently pulled the left leg out a little, again gently, shifting the guy's head, onto the side: and now the guy would breathe properly without the risk of choking on his tongyou. And he would have to leave it at that. It wisni cold so he wouldni die of frostbite. Leave it. You'll be aright son, he whispered and for some reason felt like kissing him on the forehead, a gesture of universal love for the suffering. We can endure, we can endure. Maybe it was a returning prophet to earth, and this was the way he had landed, on the crown of his skull and done a flaky. He laid his hand on the guy's shoulder. Ah you'll be right as rain, he said, and he got up to go. He would be though, he would be fine, you could tell, you could tell just by looking; and Peter was well-versed in that. Yet fuck sake if he hadni of known how to properly move the guy's body then he might have died, he couldve choked to death. My god but life is so fragile; truly, it is.

And he was seen. The pair of eyes watching. The gaffer was across the street. The game's a bogie. He looked to be smiling. He hated Peter so that would be the case quite clearly.

Come ower here!

Peter had walked a couple paces by then and he stopped, he looked across the road. Giuseppe Robertson was the gaffer's name. Part of his hatred for Peter was straightforward, contained in the relative weak notion of 'age'; the pair of them were of similar years and months down even to weeks perforce days and hours – all of that sort of shite before you get to the politics. Fucking bastirt. Peter stared back at him. Yeh man hey, Robertson was grinning, he was fucking grinning. Ace in the hole and three of them showing. Well well well.

Come ower here! he shouted again.

He wasnt kidding. Yeh, Peter licked his lips. He glanced sideways, the body there and still prone; Robertson seemed not to have noticed it yet. He glanced back at him and discovered his feet moving, dragging him across the road. Who was moving his fucking feet. He wasnt, it had to be someone in the prime position.

The gaffer was staring at him.

I'm sorry, said Peter.

It doesni matter about fucking sorry man you shouldni have left the job.

I had to go a place.

You had to go a place . . . mmhh; is that what you want on record?

Aye.

The gaffer grinned: You've been fun out and that's that.

As long as you put it on record.

Ah Peter Peter, so that's you at last, fucking out the door. It's taken a while, but we knew we'd get ye.

You did.

We did, aye, true, true true true, aye, we knew you'd err. So, you better collect the tab frae the office this afternoon.

Peter gazed at him, he smiled. Collect my tab?

Yes, you're finished, all fucking washed up, a jellyfish on the beach, you're done, you're in the process of evaporating. The gaffer chuckled. Your services, for what they're worth, are no longer in demand by the fathers of the city.

That's excellent news. I can retire and grow exotic plants out my window boxes.

You can do whatever the fuck you like son.

Ah, the son, I see. But Giuseppe you're forgetting, as a free man, an ordinary civilian, I can kick fuck out you and it'll no be a dismissible offence against company property.

Jovial, very jovial. And obviously if that's your wish then I'm the man, I'm game, know what I mean, game, anywhere you like Peter it's nomination time.

The two of them stared at each other. Here we have a straightforward hierarchy. Joe Robertson the gaffer and Peter the sweeper.

Fuck you and your services, muttered Peter and thereby lost the war. This was the job gone. Or was it, maybe it was just a battle: Look, said Peter, I've no even been the place yet I was just bloody going, I've no even got there.

You were just bloody going!

Aye.

You've been off the job an hour.

An hour? Who fucking telt ye that?

Never you mind.

There's a guy lying ower there man he's out the game.

So what?

I just bloody saved his life!

Robertson grinned and shook his head: Is that a fact!

That means I've just to leave him there?

Your job's taking care of the streets, he's on the fucking pavement.

Mmhh, I see.

It was on the streets, past tense.

Aw for fuck sake man look I'm sorry! And that was as far as he was going with this charade, no more, no more.

It doesni fucking matter about sorry, it's too late.

It'll no happen again yr honour ... Peter attempted a smile, a moment later he watched the gaffer leave, his bowly swagger, taking a smoke from his pocket and lighting it as he went. Death. The latest legislation. Death. Death death death. Death. Capital d e a

He continued to watch the gaffer until he turned the corner of Moir Street.

Well there were other kinds of work. They were needing sellers of a variety of stuff at primary-school gates. That was a wheeze. Why didnt he get in on that. My god, it was the coming thing. Then with a bit of luck he could branch out on his own and from there who knows, the whole of the world was available. Peter cracked himself on the back of the skull with such venemous force Aouch that he nearly knocked it off Aouch he staggered a pace, dropped his brush and clutched his head. O for fuck sake christ almighty but it was sore. He recovered, stopped to retrieve the brush.

It was bloody sore but christ that was stupid, bloody stupid thing to do, fucking eedjit – next thing he would be cutting bits out his body with a sharp pointed knife, self-mutilation, that other saviour of the working classes. O christ but the head was still nipping! My god, different if it knocked some sense into the brains but did it did it fuck.

Who had shopped him? Somebody must have. Giuseppe wouldni have been so cocky otherwise. One of the team had sold him out for a pocket of shekels; that's the fucking system boy no more street-sweeping for you. Yes boy hey, he could do anything he liked. Peter smiled and shook his head. He glanced upwards at the heavy grey clouds. He felt like putting on a shirt and tie and the good suit, and get Carol, and off they would go to a nightclub, out wining and dining the morning away. He liked night-shift. Nightshift! It was a beautiful experience. My god Robertson I'd love to fucking do you in boy that's what I would fucking like. But he had no money and he was eighteen years short of the pension. And he was not to lose control. That was all he needed. The whole of life was out to get you. There's a sentence. But it's true, true, the whole of life. Who had shopped him but for fuck sake what dirty bastirt had done the dirty, stuck the evil eye on him, told fucking Robertson the likely route. Och dear, I had a dream, I had a dream, and in this dream a man was free and could walk tall, he could walk tall, discard the brush and hold up the head, straightened shoulders and self-respect:

the guy was still lying there.

Ohhh. A whisky would be nice, a wee dram. Peter carried a hipflask on occasion but not tonight, he didnt have it tonight. Ohhh. He paused, he stared over the road, seeing the guy in that selfsame position. Perhaps he was dead, perhaps he had died during the tiff with the gaffer. Poor bastard, what was his story, we've all got them, we've all got them.

Morning has bro-ken.

Hinna Gotta . . .

SHEENA BLACKHALL

Hinna gotta bairnie
Hinna gotta lass
Hinna gotta hope 'n Hell o
Gettin any brass
Nae wirk fur young fowk
Wytin in the queue
Staunin wi the lay-affs
Hingin roon the Broo
Sez tae the cooncil
'Hae ye a hoose fur me?'
'Come back fin yer ninety
Ye'll hae priority . . .
If ye'd a timmer leg,
Or a babby in a pram,
Ye micht hae a chaunce, son
Gang hame tae yer mam.'

Mam disna wint me
It's fecht, fecht, fecht
Mebbe she wis young hersel
In eichteen echty echt

Dog-pish, hashish
Aa I wint's a hame
Jist grant me ae wish
A place tae caa ma ain
Ony kindo cubbyhole
A place tae coorie doon
Then ye widna hae tae thole
Me dossin roon the toon

Birds hae their nesties
Biggit in a tree
Gerron, mister Cooncil man
Bigg a hoose fur me!

A Night at the Pictures

(After Duhamel!) – for Sonya

TOM LEONARD

Some time ago my wife Sonya and myself went to the Glasgow Film Theatre, formerly the Cosmo. We went to see a French film called *Jean de Florette*, which had received some good reviews. Unfortunately between our house and the cinema, my wife and myself had a row. I cannot remember what it was about, or any of the details; but as we entered the cinema she delivered a particularly wounding remark, in a quiet voice. I was not going to sit having a night-out as if nothing had happened, but to storm out would have been histrionic. As the film began I therefore found that I was staring at a position on the ceiling somewhere north-west, five to eleven, of the screen itself.

The position of my head was such that a person who did not have a sight of my eyes would have assumed that I was watching the film. I did not want to disturb anyone else in the cinema by making a public issue of my estrangement from the communal event. Gradually I began to 'take in' where I was – without moving my position other than the occasional quasi-relaxational shift that would divert potential awareness in others of an unnatural rigidity in one of the group.

The dialogue that filled the theatre seemed a little harsh and loud, as if it needed some adjustment to the volume and the treble. Also the words were in French, which did not help me, as I only understand it at a simple level, spoken slowly. There were long periods without dialogue, the sound of what was perhaps a cow, of people breathing. Feet on floors, utensils, sounds that indicated a scene indoors. Voices evidently shouting from a distance meant that the action had moved once more outside. The most dramatic point was when the cinema was suddenly filled with the sound of a thunderstorm, while a man shouted at the top of his voice, then started weeping. All the while I kept my eyes averted from the screen. A couple of times my wife asked me if I was all right. I replied that I was.

Away from the screen, the quality of light that the screen threw on the walls and ceiling was surprisingly mixed, jumpy, changing all the time; I could see the varied light on the crowns of people near the front, the varying darkness at the small of their backs. Inevitably – I was in an end seat in the balcony – I could see angled shoes at the aisle's edge opposite, the usual light at the carpet shining on a man's sock at the ankle. But it was the silence that really struck me; the silence of the people around me, above all the silence of the building that was not this talking wall at which I couldn't look. The door with its sign EXIT – saying nothing. The building revealed itself as a wall of silence, literally, between the screen and the world. This is in the red light that shone faintly on my wife and myself, noticeable in the darker moments, from one of the pinlights above us.

Then it was over, and we were out. I felt I had maybe gone beyond a mark, broken a primitive taboo between friends. But to have called it the breaking of a primitive taboo would maybe have been to load it with a significance it did not deserve. After all, it had just been a huff. When asked how I had enjoyed the film, I had to admit that I had not seen any of it. But by the time we reached home, I had been told most of the story, and the row was already almost forgotten.

Months later the sequel to *Jean de Florette* – a film called *Manon des Sources* – came to the same cinema. We decided about eight o'clock one evening to go, and got to the cinema just after the film began at half-past. We were sitting in the forward region, in the last row of what is called the front section of the theatre. We were in a good mood. No question of a huff tonight.

After a short while my wife remarked that the opening seemed to be the same as the last one. I thought that perhaps this was a runthrough, a kind of reminder of what had taken place in Part One. Or else it was employing the device of beginning and ending the film with the same images, to make some artistic point – like Polanski's *Repulsion*, or the sound of the carcrash in Losey's *Accident*. But this was not the case. It was simply that for the benefit of those who had not seen the film before, the cinema was showing *Jean de Florette*, today, Wednesday. The sequel *Manon de Sources* would be shown on Thursday, Friday and Saturday. We had made a mistake.

But my wife had enjoyed the film on its first showing, and she generously agreed that we should just sit there again. So the sounds that had formed for me an incomprehensible abstract were now united with their visual images. I was a member of the audience with my companion, and saw nothing of what I had seen so stealthily before.

Near Linton Burnfoot

RON BUTLIN

Tarred roads, metal cattle-grids and wheeltracks mesh
so tightly no land can escape; tractor ruts
cut deep into the grass to cross and double-stitch
the fields together; where the high ground pushes upwards,
pylons rigid with electricity stand guard
upon the hills. Bridges staple running water,
lines of fence-posts nail the valley sides in place.

Rain and ploughed mud. Rooks' cries claw the air;
a banshee trapped in corrugated iron, shrieks
to be released. Trees grasp at nothing and let go
– a thousand masts rammed deep into one deck, and yet
the countryside remains becalmed. It is a scene
a child has painted splashing colours on sodden paper;
his carelessness might tear a mountainside apart.

The shingle grinding to nothing on the riverbed,
the clouds' silence soaking into the hills
– these are secrets I dare not tell
even to myself; they weight each moment of my life.

Bizarre Situations

WILLIAM BOYD

Before we start, something from this book I'm reading, called *Truth, Falsehood and Philosophy:*

> It occasionally happens that a situation is so new and unusual that no speaker of the language is equipped to say what words are appropriate for it. We shall call such situations *bizarre.*

That's what the book says, and I think it's quite interesting and fairly relevant. But, how to begin? Perhaps:

> I shall never forget the sight of Joan's crumpled body, her head clumsily de-topped like a fractious child's attempt to open a boiled egg; as if some giant's teaspoon had levered and battered its way to Joan's decidedly average brain.

Or maybe:

> I am here in Paris, Monday night, Bar Cercle, Rue Christine – well into my third Pernod – looking for Kramer. Kramer who came to stay and allowed his wife to suicide in my guest bedroom. Suicide? No chance. Kramer murdered her and I have the proof. I think.

Or possibly:

> To cure some chronic cases of epilepsy surgeons sometimes resort to a severance of the *corpus callosum*, the substance that holds together – and forms a crucial link between – the two hemispheres of the brain. The cure is radical, as is all brain surgery, but on the whole completely successful. Except, that is, for some very unusual side effects.

Into which we shall go later – my own epilepsy has been cured in this way. But, to return, the problem now is that all the beginnings are very apt, very apt indeed. Three of them though: three routes leading God knows where. And then, endings too are equally important, for – really – what I'm after is the truth. Or even TRUTH. A very elusive character. As elusive as bloody Kramer, sod him.

My preoccupation with truth arises from the division of my *corpus callosum* and explains why I am reading this book called *Truth, Falsehood and Philosophy*. I open at random. Chapter Two: Expressing Beliefs in Sentences. 'Beliefs are hard to study directly and many sentences do not naturally state beliefs . . .' My eyes dart impatiently down the page, '. . . although truth does *not* have degrees it *does* have many borderline cases.' At last something pertinent. For someone with my unique problems these donnish evasions and qualifications are incredibly frustrating. So, 'truth has borderline cases'. Good, I'm glad to find the academics admit this much, especially as since my operation the whole world has become a borderline case for me.

Kramer was at school with me. To be candid I admired him greatly and he casually exploited my admiration. In fact you could say that I loved Kramer – in a brotherly sort of way – to such an extent that, had he bothered to ask, I would have laid down my life for him. It sounds absurd to admit this now, but there was something almost noble about Kramer's disregard for everyone except himself. You know these selfish people whose selfishness seems quite reasonable, admirable, really, in its refusal to compromise. Kramer was like that: intelligent, mysterious and self-absorbed.

We were at university together for a while, but he was scandalously sent-down and went off to America where he duly made something of a name for himself as a sort of hoodlum art critic; a cultural vigilante with no respect for reputations. I often saw shadowy photographs of him in fashionable glossy magazines, and it was in one of them that I learned of his marriage – after ten years of rampant bachelorhood – to one Joan Aslinger, heiress to a West Coast fast-food chain.

Kramer and I had grown to become close friends of a sort and I continued to write to him regularly. I'm happy to report that he kept in touch: the odd letter, kitsch postcards from Hammamet or Tijuana. He used to come and stay as well – with his current girlfriend whoever that might be – in my quiet Devon cottage for a boisterous weekend every two years or so.

I remember he was surprisingly solicitous when he heard about my operation and in an uncharacteristic gesture of largesse sent a hundred white roses to the clinic where I was convalescing. He promised shortly to visit me with his new wife Joan.

It was during one of my periodic sojourns in the Sanatorium that I experienced the particularly acute and destructive epileptic attack which prompted the doctors to recommend the severing of my *corpus callosum*. The operation was a complete success. I remember only waking up as bald as a football with a thin livid stripe of lacing running fore and aft along my skull.

The surgeon – a Mr Berkeley, a genial elderly Irishman – did mention the unusual side effects I would have as a result of the *coupage* but dismissed them with a benign smile as being 'metaphysical' in character and quite unlikely to impair the quality of my daily life. Foolishly, I accepted his assurances.

Kramer and his wife came to stay as promised. Joan was a fairly attractive girl; she had delightful honey-blonde hair – always so clean – bright blue eyes and a loose generous mouth. She chatted and laughed in what was clearly an attempt at sophisticated animation, but it was immediately obvious to me that she was hopelessly neurotic and quite unsuited to be Kramer's wife. When they were together the tension that crackled between them was unbearable. On the first night they stayed I overheard a savage teeth-clenched row in the guest bedroom.

It was the effect on Kramer that I found most depressing. He was drawn and cowed, like a cornered beaten man. His brilliant wit was reduced to glum monosyllables or fervent contradictions of any opinion Joan ventured to express. Irritation and despair were lodged in every feature of his face.

It didn't surprise me greatly when, three strained days later, Kramer announced that he had to go to London on business and Joan and I found ourselves with a lot of time on our hands. She tried hard, I have to admit, but I found her tedious and dull, as most obsessively introspective people tend to be. She came slightly more alive when she drank, which was frequently, and our preprandial lunchtime session swiftly advanced to elevenses.

I soon got the full story of Kramer's constant bastardy of course: a tearful, finger-knotting account leaden with self-pity that went on well into the night. Other women apparently, from the word go. Things had become dramatically worse because now, it seemed, there was one in particular; one Erica – said with much venom – an old flame. As Erica's description emerged I realised to my surprise that I knew her. She had figured in two of Kramer's visits before his marriage to Joan. Erica was a tall intelligent red-head, strong-shouldered and of arresting appearance and with a calm and confident personality. I had liked her a lot. Naturally I didn't tell any of this to Joan whom – as Kramer predictably rang from London announcing successive delays – I was beginning to find increasingly tiresome; she was getting on my nerves.

Take her reaction to my own particular case, for example. When I explained my unique problems caused by the side effects of my operation, she didn't believe me. She laughed, said I must be joking, claimed that such things could never happen. I admitted such cases were exceptionally rare but affirmed it as documented medical fact.

I now know, thanks to this book I'm reading, the correct academic term for my 'ailment'. I am a 'bizarre situation'. Reading on I find this conclusion:

> Our language is not sufficiently articulated to cope with such rare and unusual circumstances. Many philosophers and logicians are deeply unhappy about 'bizarre situations'.

So, even the philosophers have to admit it. In my case there is no hope of ever reaching the truth. I find the concession reassuring somehow – but I still feel that I have to see Kramer again.

Indeed, my condition is truly bizarre. Since the link between my cerebral hemispheres was severed my brain now functions as two discrete halves. The only bodily function that this affects is perception, and the essence of the problem is this. If I see, for example, a cat in my *left*-side area of vision and I am asked to write down what I have seen with my *right*-hand – I am right-handed – I cannot. I cannot write down what I have seen because the right half of my brain no longer registers what occurred in my left-hand area of vision. This is because the hemispherical division in your brain extends, so to speak, the length of your body. Right hemisphere controls right side, left hemisphere left side. Normally the information from both sides has free passage from one hemisphere to the other – linking the two halves into one unified whole. But now that this route – the *corpus callosum* – has gone, only *half* my brain has seen the cat, the right hemisphere knows nothing about it so it can hardly tell my right hand what to note down.

This is what the surgeon meant by 'metaphysical' side effects, and he was right to say my day-to-day existence would be untroubled by them, but consider the radical consequences of this on my phenomenological world. It is now nothing but a sequence of *half* truths. What, for me, is really true? How can I be sure if something that happens in my left-side area of vision really took place, if in one half of my body there is *absolutely no record of it ever having occurred?*

I spend befuddled hours wrestling with these arcane epistemological riddles. Doubt is underwritten; it comes to occupy a superior position to truth and falsehood. I am a genuine, physiologically real sceptic – medically consigned to this fate by the surgeon's knife. Uncertainty is the only thing I can really be sure of.

You see what this means, of course. In my world truth is exactly what I want to believe.

I came to this book hoping for some sort of guidance, but it can only bumble on about the 'insufficient articulation of our language', which is absolutely no help at all, however accurate it may be. For example, the door of this café I'm sitting in is on my left-hand side. I clearly see in my left field of vision a tall woman in black come through it and advance towards the bar. I take a pen from my pocket and intend to write down what I saw in the margin of my book. I say to myself: 'Write down what you saw coming through the door.' I cannot do it, of course. As far as the right-hand side of my body is concerned the lady in black does not exist. So which hemisphere of my brain do I trust, then? Which version of the truth do I accept; lady or no lady?

They are both true as far as I am concerned, and whatever I decide one half of my body will back my judgment to the death.

Of course there is a simple way out: I can turn round, bring her into my right field of vision, firmly establish her existence. But that's entirely up to me. Oh yes. Unlike the rest of you, verification is a gift I can bestow or withdraw at will.

I turn. I see her. She is tall, with curly reddish auburn hair. Our eyes meet, part, meet again. Recognition flares. It is Erica.

It was I who discovered Joan's body on the floor of the guest bedroom. (One shot: my father's old Smith and Wesson pressed against her soft palate. I use the revolver – fully licensed of course – to blast at the rooks which sometimes wheel and caw round the house. Indeed, Joan and I spent a tipsy afternoon engaged in this sport. I couldn't have known . . .)

Kramer was still in London. I had gone out to a dinner party leaving Joan curled up with a whisky bottle – she had muttered something about a migraine. Naturally, I phoned the police at once.

Kramer arrived on the first train from London the next morning, numbed and shattered by the news.

At the inquest – a formality – it came out that Joan had attempted suicide a few months earlier and Kramer admitted to the rockiness of their marriage. He stayed with me until it was all over. They were stressful edgy days. Kramer was taciturn and preoccupied which, under the circumstances, wasn't surprising. He did tell me, though, that he hadn't been continually in London but in fact had spent some days in Paris with Erica where some sort of emotional crisis had ensued. He had only been back thirty-six hours when the police phoned his London hotel with the news of Joan's death.

And now Erica herself sits opposite me. Her face has very little make-up on and she looks tense and worried. After the initial pleasantries we both blurt out, 'What are you doing here?' and both realise simultaneously that we are here for the same reason. Looking for Kramer.

When Kramer left after the inquest he told me he was going to Paris to rejoin Erica and make a film on De Chirico for French TV. Apparently unperturbed he had continued to sleep in the guest bedroom but it was several days before I could bring myself to go in and clean it out. In the waste-paper basket I found several magazines, a map of Paris, a crumpled napkin from the Bar Cercle with the message 'Monday, Rue Christine' scrawled on it and, to my alarm and intense consternation, a semi-transparent credit card receipt slip from a filling station on the M4 at a place no more than a hour's drive from the house. This unsettled me. As far as I knew Kramer had no car. And, what was more disturbing, the date on the receipt slip was the same as the night Joan died.

Erica is distinctly on edge. She says she has arranged to meet Kramer here tonight as she has something to tell him. She picks at her lower lip distractedly.

'But anyway,' she says with vague annoyance, 'what do you want him for?'

I shrug my shoulders. 'I have to see him as well,' I say. 'There's something I have to clear up.'

'What is it?'

I almost tell her. I almost say, I want the truth. I want to know if he killed his wife. If he hired a car, drove to the house, found her alone and insensibly drunk, typed the note, put the pistol in her lolling mouth and blew the top of her head off.

But I don't. I say it's just a personal matter.

There is a pause in our conversation. I say to Erica, who nervously lights a cigarette, 'Look, I think I should talk to him first.'

'No!' she replies instantly. 'I must speak to him.' Speak to him about what? I wonder. It irritates me. Is Kramer to be hounded perpetually by these neurotic harpies? What has the man done to deserve this?

We see Kramer the same time as he sees us. He strides over to our table. He stares angrily at me.

'What the hell are you doing here?' he demands in tones of real astonishment.

'I'm sorry,' I say, nervousness making my voice tremble. 'But I have to speak to you.' It's like being back at school.

Erica crushes out her cigarette and jumps to her feet. I can see she is blinking back tears.

'I have news for you,' she says, fighting to keep her voice strong. 'Important news.'

Kramer grips her by the elbows. 'Come back,' he says softly, pleading.

I am impatient with whatever lovelorn drama it is that they are enacting, and also obscurely angered by this demeaning display of reliance. Raising my voice I flourish the credit card receipt. 'Kramer,' I say, 'I want to know about this.'

He ignores me. He does not take his eyes from Erica. 'Erica, please,' he entreats.

She lowers her head and looks down at her shaking hands.

'No,' she says desperately. 'I can't. I'm marrying Jean-Louis. I said I would tell you tonight. Please let me go.' She shakes herself free of his arms and brushes past him out into the night. I am glad to see her go.

I have never seen a man look so abject. Kramer stands with his head bowed in defeat, his jaw muscles bulging, his eyes fixed – as if he's just witnessed some dreadful atrocity. I despise him like this, so impoverished and vulnerable, nothing like the Kramer I knew.

I lean forward, 'Kramer,' I say softly, confidingly. 'You can tell me now. You did it, didn't you? You came back that night while I was away.' I spread the slip of transparent paper on the table. 'You see I have the facts here.' I keep my voiced low. 'But don't worry, it's between you and me. I just need to know the truth.'

Kramer sits down unsteadily. He examines the receipt. Then he looks up at me as if I'm quite mad.

'Of course I came back,' he whispers bitterly. 'I drove back that night to tell Joan I was leaving her, that I wanted Erica.' He shakes his head in grim irony. 'Instead I saw everything. From the garden. I saw you sitting in your study. You had a kind of bandage round your head. It covered one eye.' He points to my right eye. 'You were typing with one hand. Your left hand. You only used one hand. All the time. I saw you take the gun from the drawer with your left hand.' He paused. 'I knew what you were going to do. I didn't want to stop you.' He stands up. 'You are a sick man,' he says, 'with your sick worries. You can delude yourself perhaps, but nobody else.' He looks at me as if he can taste vomit in his mouth. 'I stood there and listened for the shot. I went along with the game. I share the guilt. But it was you who did it.' He turns and walks out of the café.

KRAMER IS LYING. It is a lie. The sort of mad impossible fantastic lie a desperate man would dream up. I know he is lying because I know the truth. It's locked in my brain. It is inviolate. I have my body's authority for it.

Still, there is a problem now with this lie he's set loose. Mendacity is a tenacious beast. If it's not nipped in the bud it's soon indistinguishable from the truth. I told him he didn't need to worry. But now . . .

He is bound to return to this melancholy bar before long. I know the banal nostalgia of such disappointed men – haunting the sites of their defeats – and the powerful impulses of unrequited love. I will have to see Kramer again; sort things out once and for all.

I signal the waiter for my bill. As I close my book a sentence at the bottom of the page catches my eye:

> Many logicians and philosophers are deeply unhappy about bizarre situations.

A curse on them all I say.

The Celtic Saints

ROBERT CRAWFORD

One twirls a shamrock to explain the Trinity, another
Exorcises a sea-serpent;

Coracling everywhere, spinning round
In their offshore dodgems, banging into gales

Near Lismore or Greenland, birled like Celtic knots,
Their journeys are doodled by God, pushing out

From the Hebrides of themselves – their cells
Made of strong skin, like the body

Avoiding the devil, singing endlessly
Into the endless, praising running water

For its non-stop; their medieval Latin
Is light and hymnlike, a Pictish whisper

Taking the form of an Irish wolfhound
That courses the hills from another mirrory loch

Still undiscovered, with its small green island, its ringing
Bronze quadrangular bell.

Birthright

WILMA MURRAY

Donald puts down the phone and swears. His wife raises her eyebrows without taking her eyes off the TV propped at the end of the breakfast bar.

'Problems?'

'It's the old dear. She's wandered off.'

'How can that happen? They're supposed to be supervised in those places. Surely?'

'Well, she's missing. The matron remembers her saying last night that she was going home for a little while and she must have just taken off early this morning. They didn't take it seriously, of course. Well, you know what half of them are like in there.'

'You'd better phone the house, then. See she's all right. Has she got keys?'

Donald nods while dialling the number. He waits, his body strict with irritation. 'God, what a pain. Oh, come on!' He growls into the instrument but it refuses him a reply. 'She's either not there, or not answering. Conn. He's nearer. He can take a look round.' He dials again. 'Look at the time. I'm late already.'

'She will go back? To the Home, I mean, won't she, Donald?'

'Of course.'

'I'm not having her here again. She's far too much work now.'

'I know. I know.'

'Conn can take her this time. She's his mother, too, I've done my . . .'

'I know. Oh, Conn? Hello. Look, Mother's wandered off from the Home. They've just phoned, but she could have been gone for a while. Yes. They've looked all round the place and they think maybe she's gone to the house. Could you look in and call me back? Hell, I know what time it is. But you're nearer. I have work, too, you know. Oh, sod it, then, I'll go myself.' He clatters the phone down. 'Bloody big shot.'

'Should I phone Carly, Donald?' She could maybe help, too.'

'Please yourself. I'm off. Phone work for me.'
The old woman on the country bus is clutching a big old handbag to her chest and muttering to herself. The other passengers are exchanging looks and the driver keeps checking on her in his mirror. Suddenly, she gets up and wants the bus to stop at a gate into a wood. The driver has to leave his seat to help her down.

'Are you sure this is where you want to get off, love?'

'Sure as I'm standing here. Family.' She smiles and nods towards the wood. 'It's a shortcut.'

'You'll be okay?'

'Yes, thank you. You're very kind.'

'You're sure now? Is there somebody waiting for you?'

She smiles and nods towards the wood again. 'Family.'

'All right, love. Take care, then.'

She begins a tuneless humming as she opens the gate. The path she walks is canopied by ancient branches making black lace against the sky. She stops to look up. 'Listen, now. Listen, girl.' She stands dwarfed in the cathedral of beeches, her head tilted sideways, listening. 'The same old songs,' she says and moves on, smiling.

In her house, the house she will not sell, let, or, it sometimes seems to them, even think about, Donald is phoning home. 'She's not here. Hasn't been here, either, by the look of it. Shouldn't we call the police? After all, you know what she's like. Up at half-past six. She's had a couple of hours start on us already. Okay, I'll hold on here for a while. I expect you're right.'

The house is uncomfortably quiet and lifeless without the cats, the dog and his mother's maddening tuneless humming. A fine dust has dulled the skin of every surface; noises bounce back out of empty corners stripped of the ornaments which was all she wanted with her; even his own footsteps startle him. Outside, the garden has struggled through a careless spring to show off daffodils in untidy clumps. The greenhouse has been completely shaded out by an unpruned holly tree and inside it things lie brittle and neglected in toppled pots. The phone ringing makes him jump. He runs back inside.

'Carly? Your mum's told you about Grandma, then? No, I'm just waiting here. I'm not sure what else I can do. What do you mean? What other house? Oh, I see. No, I can't go. I don't even know where it is, except it's somewhere at the back of beyond. You do? How come? I see. You never told us. When was this? Okay, okay, if you like. But if she doesn't turn up soon, it'll have to be a police job. I'm going to phone them now, anyway. See you.' Just as he is putting the phone down, he snatches it back up again. 'What was it called, that place? Carly?' he shouts down the receiver. 'Gone. God, I should know. She spoke about it often enough,' he tells the purring receiver.

He stares across the sink to the garden, drumming his fingers on the worktop. 'Photographs!' he suddenly announces with a drum roll on the side of the sink.

In the dining-room he grabs open the sideboard drawer and pulls out the well-worn box. A life's record is scattered on the table, making a crazy kaleidoscope of time, a grey mass speckled with bright colours from his own more recent life and times. He picks up one or two at random, as though about to start a jigsaw, then abandons the pile.

The old woman is resting on a tree stump, one shoe shuffling a debris of old beech-mast. Some are blackened by age, some still autumn brown, but most are splayed into brittle flowers, their perfect geometry undone. She picks at one still closed and prises out the sleek brown nuts into her palm. She chews on one and studies a tiny curled fern frond growing from a crack in the stump just beside her knee. She pulls the frond straight, gently, lets it go and smiles as it curls up again. In front of her the ground is spattered with the white stars of the wood anemones and the tender green trefoils of wood sorrel not yet in flower. She sits until her breathing is even.

Donald hears the door being rattled and almost runs into the hall. 'Mother? Oh, it's you, Conn. I thought you had to get to work. Big boss and all that.'

'No sign?'

'No.'

'What's all this?' He picks up a few of the photographs from the heap on the draining board and studies them. 'I don't know half these folk. Do you? God, there must be about a century's photographs here. Some of these could be worth something. Hey! That's your wedding photo. Look at the suit!'

'And this one's Conn with his little baby curls.' They grin, seeing themselves as they were.

'What've you got all this lot out for, anyway?'

'Carly thought . . . mind you, it's a bit wild, but you know Carly . . . that when Mother said she was going home, she could have meant her own home. Where she was born and brought up, you see? I just thought I might find some clue in this lot. That's all.'

'Her granny's place? What was it called? Some weird name.'

'Did she ever take *you* there, Conn?'

'Nope.'

'Me neither. She took Carly, though, it seems. Carly's on her way over now. She could show us the way.'

'A bit unlikely, isn't it, though? Her going back to wherever it was?'

'That's what I thought. But Carly wants to help. And they're pretty close those two, you know.'

'What did Mother take with her? Do we know?'

'Only her coat, hat and the handbag, of course.'

'Oh, well. That's it, then, Donald my old son. She could go anywhere with the travelling safe.'

'Do you think she's going . . . you know, dottled?'

'Looks like it.'

'God.'

Conn studies the garden, shoulder to shoulder with his brother. 'Any booze in the house?'

'Doubt it. Apart from her famous rodden wine, of course. There's bottles of it under the stairs.'

'No thanks.' Conn picks up another photograph. 'Look at this lot. Who were they, do you imagine? The staff of some country house?'

'Well, Mother's whole family worked for some laird. Probably some of them there, in fact. Not that I'd know.'

'All that cool, starched linen, eh? Dinky little maids bringing in your shaving water and all that. Those were the days, right enough.' He picks up another one, a sepia print of a rather severe old lady. 'Do you think this could be the old dear's granny, then?'

'No idea.'

'How come she was brought up by her granny, anyway? Some dark family scandal?'

'I'm not sure. I just know she was illegitimate. Some hush-up job, I imagine.'

'Don't you ever wonder about it?'

'Not really. What's the point?'

'The family tree, man. Bloody great branches missing.'

'There are always records of these things if you really get keen enough to find out. Mind you, "Father – Not Known" is probably all that would ever have been put down on the certificate. That's what they used to do, wasn't it?'

'How the hell would I know?'

'She never told us much, did she?'

'We never asked. Anyway, it can't have been a helluva lot of fun being someone's bastard in those days.'

The little graveyard has the names of horses and dogs carved on tiny stones, set in a clearing where the grass is soft and shot through with the blue of speedwell and heart's-ease. She sets down her bag and starts to pick lichen away from the name of one of the stones.

'There you are, Brandy. Now I can see you.'

She kicks tumbled heaps of rabbit droppings away from the base until the grave is clear again. 'It's only me, Brandy. Just tidying up a bit. Nobody bothers, these days. They used to keep you all tidy in here. Poor old things. In the good old days. Aye, well. If those trees could talk, eh, Brandy?' She wanders among the stones, touching one here and there before coming back to Brandy's. Suddenly she looks up to track the flight of a pair of startled wood-pigeons. 'Ssh, now. It's okay. It's only cushies, Brandy. No boys to frighten you, now.'

'Dad? Oh, hello, Uncle Conn.' Carly bursts into the house, a jumble of bright colours, her face painted in shades of mauve. 'Any sign?'

'Fraid not.'

'I told you I didn't think she'd be here. She never liked this house, you know. Lived in it for fifty years and never liked it. That's really sad, isn't it?'

'How come you know all this, missy?'

'Grandma tells me a lot of things. I could listen to her stories all day. Last time I visited her, in that *awful* place, she was going on about the old house again. About the trees and the flowers and all that kind of stuff. All the stuff nobody cares about any more, right? Making her rodden wine. You know. Anyway, I promised I'd take her there when I got my new car and I didn't. Now I feel awful. So you see, I think that's where she's gone.'

'But Carly, old folk are always going on about the old days. They remember them more clearly than last week, say.'

'Dad. She's not senile. She even jokes about that. Says she will soon have to look at the nameplate on her door to see who she is. I think, actually, joking about it is a really good way to cope with it, you know? Look, are we going, or not?'

The bank below the old house is thick with bluebells, blue, white and pink bluebells. She reaches up the bank and picks a fat bunch, letting their strings of saliva leak all down her brown coat. 'Blue for a boy.'

The last part of the path to the house is steeper than she can manage comfortably and she has to rest against the old rowan tree when she finally gets to it, to recover her breath. 'I'm getting old, right enough.' She leans her cheek against the bark and looks up into the branches. Buds are just bursting, the leaves still folded into tiny fans. 'The leaves must be late this year. They were well out, that day. It was your own fault you fell, you know. Your own fault for showing off.' With pain in her face, she gets down on her knees and lays the bluebells on the grass. 'Anyway, peace. You'd be an old man now, nearly as old as me. Probably dottled as well. And you didn't know any better. You were just a child. A boy, a spoiled little boy. You couldn't help having *him* for a father, any more than I could. Him and his Sunday pennies!' She pulls herself up awkwardly and turns away towards the house, brushing at the marks on her coat.

'I would have liked to dance at your wedding, though,' she calls back over her shoulder.

'How could she get as far as here?'

'Oh, she used to come here often on the bus by herself. To have a wander round. We'll have to leave the car here, by the way, if we want to do her walking tour.'

'This is some sort of estate by the look of it. I'm not sure we should even be here, Carly. Who lives here? In the house?'

'Nobody, now, so we've as much right as anyone. Look! That's the chestnut tree she got her conkers from. She used to hoard the green spiky balls to pelt the laird's son when he came home from his fancy school for the summer. Then she used to run away and climb right up to the top of that tree there. He was a right coward. He couldn't climb trees. Oh, and look, that's the paddock where she kept her Shetland pony, Brandy. The house is just up the hill and round the corner. The pony was a present from the laird, but Brandy was old and probably not worth much. All these garages used to be stables. She saw her first car here and the laird used to roll pennies down the ramp to her, if she was playing there when he was getting the car out for church.'

'Why did he do that?'

'I don't know, do I?'

'She sounds like a real odd-ball of a kid, Conn.'

'Well, come on, let's face it, Donald. She was an odd-ball of a mother. "Boys! Nasty things, boys," she used to say. That's your advantage, Carly, being a girl.'

'Oh, that's hardly fair, Uncle Conn. I know she's a bit eccentric sometimes, but she's really interested in things. Modern things, ideas even.'

'Like what, for example?'

'Women's rights, that sort of thing. Abortion, even. She approves of that, women being able to choose. We had a long talk about it, as a matter of fact.'

'More like *you* had a long talk about it. God, Carly, I sometimes wish you weren't so intense about things. It tires me out. God knows what it does to your grandma.'

'The house is just up here. There she is! I told you she'd be here!'

She is sitting on the front steps of a derelict house, leaning back against the peeling wooden door. She looks at Carly from a long way away behind her eyes, it seems. 'Carly? Granny's gone, Carly. They're all gone. Dead and buried.'

'I know, Grandma.'

'Oh, Carly. I'm so tired.'

'What have you been doing?'

'Just remembering things. I'm tired now.'

'It's okay. We're here to take you back. Dad and Conn are here, too, see?'

'The boys? What are *they* doing here?'

'We've been looking for you, Mother. We've been looking for you all morning.'

'Why? I told the matron. I told her I had to go home. I'm sure I did. Didn't I?'

'Yes you did, Grandma. You did. Come on, I'll help you up. We'll get you back. Dad, go and get the car.'

In the car, the old woman leans her head against the back of the seat and shuts her eyes. They drive back the way they came, silent now.

'He used to call me a tink,' she says suddenly.

'Who did?' Donald asks.

'The laird's son. But I wasn't a tink. I was as good as him any day. Granny always told me to remember that.'

'Of course you were, Grandma.'

In the back seat of the car, Carly is stroking her grandmother's shiny, wrinkled hands.

'Poor old soul, I must have been such a worry to her.'

Donald turns his attention from the road to look at Conn. 'So, what's new, eh?' he asks, very softly.

Depths

STEWART CONN

Wakened in the small hours
by a dull clang (too early
for the binmen) I find
sleep dispelled, by sounds
of a different kind.

Buckets are being filled
at the head of the byre;
accompanying the splash
of water, a rhythmic swish
of hard bristle, down the gutter.

Then something else
I do not want to hear;
a series of plaintive squeals,
accompanied by others
less high-pitched, yet sharper.

Alone in a chill dawn,
I listen to a muscovy cat tear
with her claws at the sliding door
as in the great tub, I hold down
the sack in which her kittens drown.

Being Frank

IAN RANKIN

It wasn't easy, being Frank.

That's what everybody called him, when they weren't calling him a dirty old tramp or a scrounger or a layabout. Frank, they called him. Only the people at the hostel and at the Social Security bothered with his full name: Francis Rossetti Hyslop. Rossetti, he seemed to remember, not after the painter but after his sister the poet, Christina. Most often, a person – a person in authority – would read that name from the piece of paper they were holding and then look up at Frank, not quite in disbelief, but certainly wondering how he'd come so low.

He couldn't tell them that he was climbing higher all the time. That he preferred to live out of doors. That his face was weatherbeaten, not dirty. That a plastic bag was a convenient place to keep his possessions. He just nodded and shuffled his feet instead, the shuffle which had become his trademark.

'Here he comes,' his companions would cry. 'Here comes The Shuffler!' Alias Frank, alias Francis Rossetti Hyslop.

He spent much of the spring and autumn in Edinburgh. Some said he was mad, leaving in the summer months. That, after all, was when the pickings were richest. But he didn't like to bother the tourists, and besides, summer was for travelling. He usually walked north, through Fife and into Kinross or Perthshire, setting up camp by the side of a loch or up in the hills. And when he got bored, he'd move on. He was seldom moved on by gamekeepers or the police. Some of them he knew of old, of course. But others he encountered seemed to regard him more and more as some rare species, or, as one had actually said, a 'national monument'.

It was true, of course. Tramp meant to walk and that's what tramps used to do. The term 'gentleman of the road' used to be accurate. But the tramp was being replaced by the beggar: young, fit men who didn't move from the city and who were unrelenting in their search for spare change. That had never been Frank's way. He had his regulars of course, and often he only had to sit on a bench in The Meadows, a huge grassy plain bordered by tree-lined paths, and wait for the money to appear in his lap.

That's where he was when he heard the two men talking. It was a bright day, a lunchtime and there were few spaces to be had on the meagre supply of Meadows benches. Frank was sitting on one, arms folded, eyes closed, his legs stretched out in front of him with one foot crossed over the other. His three carrier-bags were on the ground beside him, and his hat lay across his legs – not because he was hot especially, but because you never knew who might drop a coin in while you were dozing, or pretending to doze.

Maybe his was the only bench free. Maybe that's why the men sat down beside him. Well, 'beside him' was an exaggeration. They squeezed themselves on to the furthest edge of the bench, as far from him as possible. They couldn't be comfortable, squashed up like that and the thought brought a moment's smile to Frank's face.

But then they started to talk, not in a whisper but with voices lowered. The wind, though, swept every word into Frank's right ear. He tried not to tense as he listened, but it was difficult. Tried not to move, but his nerves were jangling.

'It's war,' one said. 'A council of war.'

War? He remembered reading in a newspaper recently about terrorists. Threats. A politician had said something about vigilance. Or was it vigilantes? A council of war: it sounded ominous. Maybe they were teasing him, trying to scare him from the bench so that they could have it for themselves. But he didn't think so. They were speaking in undertones; they didn't think he could hear. Or maybe they simply knew that it didn't matter whether an old tramp heard them or not. Who would believe him?

This was especially true in Frank's case. Frank believed that there was a worldwide conspiracy. He didn't know who was behind it, but he could see its tentacles stretching out across the globe. Everything was connected, that was the secret. Wars were connected by arms manufacturers, the same arms manufacturers who made the guns used in robberies, who made the guns used by crazy people in America when they went on the rampage in a shopping-centre or hamburger restaurant. So already you had a connection between hamburgers and dictators. Start from there and the thing just grew and grew.

And because Frank had worked this out, he wondered from time to time if *they* were after him. The dictators, the arms industry, or maybe even the people who made the buns for the hamburger chains. Because he *knew*. He wasn't crazy; he was sure of that.

'If I was,' he told one of his regulars, 'I wouldn't wonder if I was or not, would I?'

And she'd nodded, agreeing with him. She was a student at the university. A lot of students became regulars. They lived in Tollcross, Marchmont, Morningside, and had to pass through The Meadows on their way to the university buildings in George Square. She was studying psychology, and she told Frank something.

'You've got what they call an active fantasy life.'

Yes, he knew that. He made up lots of things, told himself stories. They whiled away the time. He pretended he'd been an RAF pilot, a spy, minor royalty, a slave-trader in Africa, a poet in Paris. But he *knew* he was making all these stories up, just as he knew that there really was a conspiracy.

And these two men were part of it.

'Rhodes,' one of them was saying now.

A council of war in Rhodes. So there was a Greek connection, too. Well, that made sense. He remembered stories about the generals and their junta. The terrorists were using Greece as their base. And Edinburgh was called the 'Athens of the north'. Yes! Of course! That's why they were basing themselves in Edinburgh too. A symbolic gesture. Had to be.

But who would believe him? That was the problem, being Frank. He'd told so many stories in the past, given the police so much information about the conspiracy, that now they just laughed at him and sent him on his way. Some of them thought he was looking for a night in the cells and once or twice they'd even obliged, despite his protests.

No, he didn't want to spend another night locked up. There was only one thing for it. He'd follow the men and see what he could find. Then he'd wait until tomorrow. They were talking about tomorrow, too, as if it was the start of their campaign. Well, tomorrow was Sunday and with a bit of luck if Frank hung around The Meadows, he'd bump into another of his regulars, one who might know exactly what to do.

Sunday morning was damp, blustery. Not the sort of day for a constitutional. This was fine by John Rebus: it meant there'd be fewer people about on Bruntsfield Links. Fewer men chipping golf-balls towards his head with a wavering cry of 'Fore!' Talk about crazy golf! He knew the Links had been used for this purpose for years and years, but all the same there were so many paths cutting through that it was a miracle no one had been killed.

He walked one circuit of the Links, then headed as usual across Melville Drive and into The Meadows. Sometimes he'd stop to watch a kickabout. Other times, he kept his head down and just walked, hoping for inspiration. Sunday was too close to Monday for his liking and Monday always meant a backlog of work. Thinking about it never did any good, of course, but he found himself thinking of little else.

'Mr Rebus!'

But then The Meadows offered other distractions, too.

'Mr Rebus!'

'Hello, Frank.'

'Sit yourself down.'

Rebus lowered himself on to the bench. 'You look excited about something.'

Frank nodded briskly. Though he was seated, he shuffled his feet on the earth, making little dance movements. Then he looked around him, as though seeking interlopers.

Oh no, thought Rebus, here we go again.

'War,' Frank whispered. 'I heard two men talking about it.'

Rebus sighed. Talking to Frank was like reading one of the Sunday rags – except sometimes the stories *he* told were more believable. Today didn't sound like one of those days.

'Talking about war? Which war?'

'Terrorism, Mr Rebus. Has to be. They've had a council of war at Rhodes. That's in Greece.'

'They were Greek, were they?'

Frank wrinkled his face. 'I don't think so. I can give you a description of them though. They were both wearing suits. One was short and bald, the other one was young, taller, with black hair.'

'You don't often see international terrorists wearing suits these days, do you?' Rebus commented. Actually, he thought to himself, that's a lie: they're becoming more smartly dressed all the time.

In any case, Frank had an answer ready. 'Need a disguise though, don't they? I followed them.'

'Did you?' A kickabout was starting nearby. Rebus concentrated on the kick-off. He liked Frank, but there were times . . .

'They went to a bed and breakfast near the Links.'

'Did they now?' Rebus nodded slowly.

'And they said it was starting *today*. Today, Mr Rebus.'

'They don't hang about, do they? Anything else?'

Frank frowned, thinking. 'Something about lavatories, or laboratories.

Must have been laboratories, mustn't it? And money, they talked about that. Money they needed to set it up. That's about it.'

'Well, thanks for letting me know, Frank. I'll keep my ears open, see if I can hear any whispers. But listen, don't go following people in future. It could be dangerous, understand?'

Frank appeared to consider this. 'I see what you mean,' he said at last, 'but I'm tougher than I look, Mr Rebus.'

Rebus was standing now. 'Well, I'd better be getting along.' He slipped his hands into his pockets. The right hand emerged again holding a pound note. 'Here you go, Frank.' He began to hand the money over, then withdrew it again. Frank knew what was coming and grinned.

'Just one question,' Rebus said, as he always did. 'Where do you go in the winter?'

It was a question a lot of his cronies asked him. 'Thought you were dead,' they'd say each spring as he came walking back into their lives. His reply to Rebus was the same as ever: 'Ah, that would be telling, Mr Rebus. That's *my* secret.'

The money passed from one hand to the other and Rebus sauntered off towards Jawbone Walk, kicking a stone in front of him. Jawbone because of the whale's jawbone which made an arch at one end of the path. Frank knew that. Frank knew lots of things. But he knew, too, that Rebus hadn't believed him. Well, more fool him. For over a year now they'd played this little game: where did Frank go in the winter? Frank wasn't sure himself why he didn't just say, I go to my sister's place in Dunbar. Maybe because it was the truth. Maybe because it *was* a secret.

Rebus looked to him like a man with secrets, too. Maybe one day Rebus would set out for a walk and never return home, would just keep on walking the way Frank himself had done. What was it the girl student had said?

'Sometimes I think we're *all* gentleman of the road. It's just that most of us haven't got the courage to take that first step.'

Nonsense: that first step was the easiest. It was the hundredth, the thousandth, the millionth that was hard. But not as hard as going back, never as hard as that.

Rebus had counted the steps to his second-floor flat many, many times. It always added up to the same number. So how come with the passing years there seemed to be more? Maybe it was the height of each step that was changing. Own up, John. For once, own up: it's *you* that's changing. You're growing older and stiffer. You never used to pause on the first-floor landing, never used to linger outside Mrs Cochrane's door, breathing in that smell unique to blackcurrant bushes and cat-pee.

How could one cat produce that amount of odour? Rebus had seen it many a time: a fat, smug-looking creature with hard eyes. He'd caught it on his own landing, turning guiltily to look at him before sprinting for the next floor up. But it was inside Mrs Cochrane's door just now. He could hear it mewling, clawing at the carpet, desperate to be outside. He wondered. Maybe Mrs Cochrane was ill? He'd noticed that recently her brass nameplate had become tarnished. She wasn't bothering to polish it any more. How old was she anyway? She seemed to have come with the tenement, almost as if they'd constructed the thing around her. Mr and Mrs Costello on the top floor had been here nigh-on twenty-five years, but they said she'd been here when they arrived. Same brass nameplate on her door. Different cat, of course, and a husband, too. Well, he'd been dead by the time Rebus and his wife – now ex-wife – had moved here, what, was it ten years ago now?

Getting old, John. Getting old. He clamped his left hand on to the banister and somehow managed the last flight of steps to his door.

He started a crossword in one of the newspapers, put some jazz on the hi-fi, drank a pot of tea. Just another Sunday. Day of rest. But he kept catching glimpses of the week ahead. No good. He made another pot of tea and this time added a dollop of J&B to the mixture in his mug. Better. And then, naturally, the doorbell rang.

Jehovah's Witnesses. Well, Rebus had an answer ready for them. A friend in the know had said that Roman Catholics are taught how to counter the persuasive arguments of the JWs. Just tell them you're a Catholic and they'll go away.

'I'm Catholic,' he said. They didn't go away. There were two of them, dressed in dark suits. The younger one stood a little behind the older one. This didn't matter, since he was a good foot taller than his elder. He was holding a briefcase. The chief, however, held only a piece of paper. He was frowning, glancing towards this. He looked at Rebus, sizing him up, then back to the paper. He didn't appear to have heard what Rebus said.

'I'm Catholic,' Rebus repeated, but hollowly.

The man shook his head. Maybe they were foreign missionaries, come to convert the heathen. He consulted his scrap of paper again.

'I think this is the wrong address,' he said. 'There isn't a Mr Bakewell here?'

'Bakewell?' Rebus started to relax. A simple mistake; they weren't JWs. They weren't salesmen or cowboy builders or tinkers. Simply, they'd got the wrong flat. 'No,' he said. 'No Mr Bakewell here. And his tart's not here either.'

Oh, they laughed at that. Laughed louder than Rebus had expected. They were still laughing as they made their apologies and started back downstairs. Rebus watched them until they were out of sight. He'd stopped laughing almost before they'd begun. He checked that his keys were in his pocket, then slammed shut his door – but with himself still out on the landing.

Their footsteps sent sibilant echoes up towards the skylight. What was it about them? If pressed, he couldn't have said. There was just *something*. The way the smaller, older man had seemed to weigh him up in a moment, then mentioned Bakewell. The way the younger man had laughed so heartily, as if it were such a release. A release of what? Tension, obviously.

The footsteps had stopped. Outside Mrs Cochrane's door. Yes, that was the ting-ting-ting of her antiquated doorbell, the kind you pulled, tightening and releasing the spring on a bell inside the door. The door which was now being pulled open. The older man spoke.

'Mrs Cochrane?' Well, they'd got that name right. But then it was on her nameplate, wasn't it? *Anyone* could have guessed at it.

'Aye.' Mrs Cochrane, Rebus knew, was not unique in making this sound not only questioning but like a whole sentence. Yes, I'm Mrs Cochrane, and who might you be and what do you want?

'Councillor Waugh.'

Councillor! No, no, there was no problem: Rebus had paid his Poll Tax, always put his bin-bags out the night before, never earlier. They might be after Bakewell, but Rebus was in the clear.

'It's about the roadworks.'

'Roadworks?' echoed Mrs Cochrane.

Roadworks? thought Rebus.

'Yes, roadworks. Digging up the roads. You made a complaint about the roads. I've come to talk to you about it.'

'Roadworks? Here, you mean?'

He was patient, Rebus had to grant him that. 'That's right, Mrs Cochrane. The road outside.'

There was a bit more of this, then they all went indoors to talk over Mrs Cochrane's grievances. Rebus opened his own door and went in, too. Then, realising, he slapped his hand against his head. These were the two men Shuffling Frank had been talking about! Of course they were, only Frank had misheard: council of war was Councillor Waugh; Rhodes was roads. What else had Frank said? Something about money; well, that might be the money for the repairs. That it was all planned to start on

Sunday: and here they were, on Sunday, ready to talk to the residents about roadworks.

What roadworks? The road outside was clear, and Rebus hadn't heard any gossip concerning work about to start. Something else Frank had heard them say. Lavatories or laboratories. Of course, his own cherished conspiracy theory had made him plump for 'laboratories', but what if he'd misheard again? Where did lavatories fit into the scheme? And if, as seemed certain, these were the two men, what was a local councillor doing staying at a bed and breakfast? Maybe he owned it, of course. Maybe it was run by his wife.

Rebus was a couple of paces further down his hall when it hit him. He stopped dead. Slow, John, slow. Blame the whisky, maybe. And Jesus, wasn't it so obvious when you thought of it? He went back to his door opened it quietly, and slipped out on to the landing.

There was no such thing as silent movement on an Edinburgh stairwell. The sound of shoe on stone, a sound like sandpaper at work, was magnified and distorted, bounding off the walls upwards and downwards. Rebus slipped off his shoes and left them on his landing, then started downstairs. He listened outside Mrs Cochrane's door. Muffled voices from the living-room. The layout of her flat was the same as Rebus's own: a long hallway off which were half-a-dozen doors, the last of which – actually around a corner – led to the living-room. He crouched down and pushed open the letterbox. The cat was just inside the door and it swiped at him with its paw. He felt the hinge fall back.

Then he tried the door handle, which turned. The door opened. The cat swept past him and down the stairs. Rebus began to feel that the odds were going his way. The door was open just wide enough to allow him to squeeze inside. Open it an inch or two further, he knew, and it creaked with the almightiest groan. He tiptoed into the hallway. Councillor Waugh's voice boomed from the living-room.

'Bowel trouble. Terrible in a man so young.'

Yes, he'd no doubt be explaining why his assistant was taking so long in the lavatory: that was the excuse they always made. Well, either that or a drink of water. Rebus passed the toilet. The door wasn't locked and the tiny closet was empty. He pushed open the next door along – Mrs Cochrane's bedroom. The young man was closing the wardrobe doors.

'Well,' said Rebus, 'I hope you didn't think *that* was the toilet.'

The man jerked around. Rebus filled the doorway. There was no way past him; the only way to get out was to go through him, and that's what the man tried, charging at the doorway, head low. Rebus stood back a little, giving himself room and time, and brought his knee up hard, aiming for the bridge of the nose but finding mouth instead. Well, it was an imprecise science, wasn't it? The man flew backwards like a discarded ragdoll and fell on to the bed. Flat out, to Rebus's satisfaction.

They'd heard the noise of course, and the 'councillor' was already on his way. But he, too, would need to get past Rebus to reach the front door. He stopped short. Rebus nodded slowly.

'Very wise,' he said. 'Your colleague's going to need some new teeth when he wakes up. I'm a police officer by the way. And you, "councillor", are under arrest.'

'Arresting the councillor?' This from Mrs Cochrane, who had appeared in the hall.

'He's no more a councillor than I am, Mrs Cochrane. He's a conman. His partner's been raking through your bedroom.'

'What?' She went to look.

'Bakewell,' Rebus said smiling. They would try the same ruse at every door where they didn't fancy their chances. Sorry, wrong address, and on to the next potential sucker until they found someone old enough or gullible enough. Rebus was trying to remember if Mrs Cochrane had a telephone. Yes, there was one in her living-room, wasn't there? He gestured to his prisoner.

'Let's go back into the living-room,' he said. Rebus could call the station from there . . .

Mrs Cochrane was back beside him. 'Blood on my good quilt,' she muttered. Then she saw that Rebus was in his stocking-soles. 'You'll get chilblains, son,' she said. 'Mark my words. You should take better care of yourself. Living on your own like that. You need somebody to look after you. Mark my words. He told me he was a councillor. Would you credit it? And me been wanting to talk to them for ages about the dog's mess on the Links.'

'Hello Shuffler.'

'Mr Rebus! Day off is it? Don't usually see you around here during the week.'

Frank was back on his bench, a newspaper spread out on his lap. One of yesterday's papers. It contained a story about some black magic conspiracy in the United States. Wealthy people, it was reckoned, influential people, taking part in orgies and rituals. Yes, and the arms manufacturers would be there, too. That's how they got to know the politicians and the bankers. It all connected.

'No, I'm off to work in a minute. Just thought I'd stop by. Here.' He was holding out a ten-pound note. Frank looked at it suspiciously, moved his hand towards it, and took it. What? Didn't Rebus even want to ask him the question?

'You were right,' Rebus was saying. 'What you told me about those two men, dead right. Well, nearly dead right. Keep your ears open, Frank. And in future, I'll try to keep *my* ears open when you talk to me.'

And then he turned and was walking away, back across the grass towards Marchmont. Frank stared at the money. Ten pounds. Enough to finance another long walk. He needed a long walk to clear his head. Now that they'd had the council of war at Rhodes, the laboratories would be making potions for satanic rituals. They'd put the politicians in a trance, and . . . No, no, it didn't bear thinking about.

'Mr Rebus!' he called. 'Mr Rebus! I go to my sister's! She lives in Dunbar! That's where I go in the winter!'

But if the distant figure heard him, it made no sign. Just kept on walking. Frank shuffled his feet. Ten pounds would buy a transistor radio, or a pair of shoes, a jacket, or a new hat, maybe a little camping stove. That was the problem with having money: you ended up with decisions to make. And if you bought anything, where would you put it? He'd need either to ditch something, or to start on another carrier-bag.

That was the problem, being Frank.

AUTHOR'S NOTE

There was a Frank, long ago when I lived in Arden Street. I'm not suggesting he's representative of the many homeless people in Scotland; he's a character, that's all. Rebus's money, however, is representative, of easy guilt, his and mine.

A Poem for Shelter

GEORGE MACKAY BROWN

Who has set his house among the stars?
Who has made his dwellingplace the
       dawn, and the western glory
       where the sun goes down?
Who has instructed the eagle to
       establish his place on a
       mountain ledge near the snow
And the little mouse in a cell safe from
       hawk and ploughshare?
The albatross dwells in the house of
       blizzard and spindrift,
       south of Cape Horn, and
       'sleeps on his own wings'.
What has Wisdom chosen, to be his
       house among men?
A byre, shared with winter creatures
But that was to set at naught
       princes' palaces and the
       pyramids of dead
       jewelled pharaohs.
The true inheritors of earth are
       the people
Who desire to live in simple houses
Not too close together but enough
       for neighbourliness
Where a family may sit at peace
       under its own rooftree.

There is enough stone in Alps, Urals,
      Himalayas
To quarry a million cornerstones.
But always, in winter, under
      stars like thorns
The wanderers wait, the breakers of icicles,
      the homeless ones.

Armageddon

VALERIE THORNTON

Armageddon sleeps in the church and lives in the park where he is walking to Sullom Voe.

The church where he sleeps is long since abandoned by all but the god on the wall. This is a Jesus, in blue and gold mosaic, high above Armageddon's head. His open arms are inviting Armageddon to be blessed. 'Come unto me' is cut into the red sandstone to his right, with 'Blessed are the poor' on his left.

When the wind whips through the ragged lace of the stained-glass windows, Armageddon curls below the hood of his mousy duffel coat, sheltering beneath the shattered ribs of the upturned organ. He knows if he uncurls and stares for long enough at the pale pointed oval on the end wall of the transept, his Jesus will materialise in the gloom and bless him, because he is poor.

Armageddon makes fairly regular sacrificial offerings to his god of polo mints, dog food and El Dorado. The polo mints are a luxury. It is enough that the god, who cannot eat, can see them. Armageddon eats them for him.

Armageddon knows the whore of Babylon lives behind lace curtains in a tenement flat opposite his church and that if he doesn't melt into his church, shadowy as the night, then the bitch will call the police.

They pick their way over the rotten floorboards, their torches staggering over the peeling walls until they pick him out and put him on the street. They're okay though. After the whore of Babylon lets fall her evening velvet curtains with a heavy rustle of self-righteousness, Armageddon walks around the block and back home again.

Armageddon belongs to the church as much as the church belongs to him. He will tell you this as you walk through his park.

He is a slight figure, pale, with fine skin drawn over his features which are sharpened by many hungers. His chin sticks out like the man in the moon, with a tiny mouth above it. Only the slightest of dark hairs above the corners of his thin lips suggest he's male. He has lost all his teeth, and his voice, light as a bird, gives nothing away.

'Bless you, Joseph!' he says, falling into step with you, however many you are, and whatever sex.

'Bless you, Joseph!' he says again, struggling to extract a new map of Scotland from the pocket of his duffel coat. 'I'm walking to Sullom Voe. It's just over there,' he says pointing in a northerly direction, towards the far side of the park. 'You been there, Joseph?'

'No, it's a bit far for me. Why are you going there?'

'I am about my father's business,' he announces, folding the map all against the preset creases and stuffing it into his pocket.

His eyes are a little sticky and there are cobwebs on the hood of his duffel coat, but his fine black hair is clean and soft.

'My name is Armageddon. I have bone in my head which doesn't belong to me. Look!'

And from his pocket he takes a grubby bird skull, small, like a thrush or blackbird. His slender pale fingers turn it this way and that, with careful knowledge of its delicacies.

'Look at it and it will be in your head too, and you will be blessed. When the circles of the years are complete, you will be on the inside too, with the rest of us. See over there, Joseph?' He points to the far side of the river, to a dark space below a mossy stone lintel, with water lapping at its lip. 'That's where I was shut behind the stone. With Mary, my mother.'

He swerves from your side to a bed of purple crocuses at the edge of the path and picks up a pebble.

'This is the same stone. It has become small with the passing of years. Soon, when the centuries turn around, it will be nothing. It is accursed from the beginning of time.'

Armageddon hurls the stone into the river.

'The trees have all been killed too,' he says.

'Yes, but they'll soon get their leaves again, in the summer, won't they?'

'Maybe, I don't know. I'm not of this time. I don't see things the way you do,' he waves his thin fingers up and down the river. 'I don't know the day or the month or the week or the decade or the season. They've taken my brain away. I'm old. Very, very old. In fact, I'm mummified. Yet underneath, I'm still wrapped in my swaddling clothes. This, my raiment, was once white.'

It's difficult to know what to say, so you say nothing.

'See that sandbank over there?' he continues.

It doesn't look like a sandbank. It's covered in last year's long grass, combed pale by the winter. It supports several leafless trees.

'When I was little my father was a carpenter. He made a basket of rushes and floated me on the river.'

'That must have been fun!'

He laughs and nods at the memory of it.

'He called me Armageddon.'

'Doesn't that mean the end of the world?'

'No, the world can't end. It says world without end.' Up ahead, leaning against the railings, staring at nothing in the river below, is an old man. His face is dark as autumn, his black clothes shabby and indistinguishable. As Armageddon draws level with him, he falls out of step and approaches the old man.

'How're you doing, Joe?' he says, offering him a polo mint.

Armageddon spends a long time, even in his timeless wilderness in the park, looking for Sullom Voe. By the time he gets back to his church, late in the evening, it has shrunk almost to nothing. There, instead of a roof to shelter below, instead of the narrow passage up to the broken way-in window, there is nothing but a big empty muddy space.

It is almost the end of the world for Armageddon, but for some reason, Jesus is still waiting for him. The transept wall, which adjoins the tenements next door, still stands, like a bookend, with a few feet of red sandstone walls on either side of Jesus, who is now opening his arms for the whole poor world to see. There is no roof, but the remainder of the wall, projecting on either side, provides some shelter. The whore of Babylon's curtains are drawn tight shut.

It is a night for Noah and by morning Armageddon is chilled to the bone. Above him, his Jesus looks over his head to the repair garage down the road, secure and smug with its white pebble-dash walls.

Armageddon, his clothes stiff with mud and many rains, is walking through the park talking to no one in particular.

'I'm a fully qualified architect, you know, Joseph. Without papers. They've taken everything away. Car, bank cards, credit cards, stocks and shares. They've taken my brain too. Left me with nothing.'

He has a fine beard curling around his chin, and his duffel coat is stained and torn. Most of his map has long gone except for the Shetland Isles which he ate.

'I have a castle in my kingdom over there,' he says, pointing south, towards the distant towers of the hospital. 'But I have to be in the wilderness now. For forty days and forty nights until Sullom Voe comes to pass. That old man's in my castle; he had a heart attack. They wouldn't have taken him in if they'd known he was related to me. No one'll take me in.'

Beside Armageddon prances a white charger, reduced to the form of a small mongrel which he is feeding with dirty polo mints.

'I am old enough to see now,' he continues, 'and I can see many homes in my head. Many little homes inside my church. For all the whores of Babylon who will be left behind when the years turn around.'

And while these things were coming to pass, Armageddon slept within the scaffolding, within the shells of flats which were rising from the ashes of the church. There was no more Jesus to come unto him, they had knocked him off the wall to make way for many bricks. But now it didn't matter. Jesus was in Armageddon's head, bright as remembrance, below the hood of his duffel coat.

When all the whores of Babylon were installed in their new quarters, when the years had turned around from the time when the poor were blessed, yet another casualty was found huddled cold as stone below his duffel coat in the park. His name was unknown, as was his age, and the message in the grey crumbs of bone and polo mint in his pocket was indecipherable.

Old Sweat, New Times
WILLIAM NEILL

No sir – it's not the first time I've slept rough.
Ground sheets and bivvie-tents and palliasses.
A long day's march and a cold night soon passes.
In those days I was hard as nails, real tough.

Pure bullshit that: 'life will be more abundant
for our brave boys who volunteered to fight.'
Medals? I sold 'em to a chap one night
right at the outset when I went redundant.

Thinking about it though: living like foxes
in holes we dug ourselves was not like this.
Knowing you might get yours was hardly bliss,
but better than dying slow in cardboard boxes.

Hame

BILLY KAY

There's a pickle words in ilka leid that canna easily be owreset –
gemütlichkeit in German, *saudade* in Portuguese – for thir's words that
belang, or puit stranger, is thirlit tae a specific culture. The word hame,
in Scots, warks for me in the same wey. The place I stey could never be
home, whaur I bide will aye be hame. I cannae imagine no haein a hame.
I think I'm strang eneuch tae thole maist o the dunts that life dings on
fowk, but hameless . . . I hae ma douts.

For ocht o the values, o the moralitie, o the sangs an music an poetry
o the steiran culture I hae inheritit aw comes frae the hame. As a Scot o
ma generation, it couldnae hae come frae onywhaur else. Frae the schuil
we got gey little o ocht that remotely belanged us. When I wes wee, the
language o hame wesnae alloued in the schuil sae like maist Scots-speakin
bairns I got a sair culture-gunk gey early on in ma education: a certificate
for recitin Rabbie Burns's poetry ae day in the year, syne skelpit wi the
tawse the ither three hunder an sixty fower days for speakin his language!
We wes an still ar, the last colony.

Wi the major cultural institutions that affected us sweirt tae acknowledge oor culture, the hame hed tae be the hert o the culture. There
ye wes tellt tae haud the heid up an be prood o wha ye wes an whaur ye
cam frae. Ye wes gien a leid, a literature, a history, a community an it wes
aw rowed thegither in yer sense o yersel in a world picture.

East's east, west's west, hame's best.

For me, hame was a pre-war cooncil hoose, for my parents whan they
first got mairrit it had been an auld slum biggin, an afore that it wes the
miners raws in Ayrshire an Fife for their mithers an faithers afore thaim.
My sisters an me mind them aw wi a lowe in the ee, for they were aw
hame. An even though it wes beginnin tae weaken in oor day, hame
wesnae juist the hoose whaur ye steyed. Hame wes neebours an freens,
an faimily skailed aw ower the toun. Yes wes tellt it wes aw yer hame in
the stories passed down.

I mindit ane recently an uised it in a play cried *Lucky's Strike* aboot a modren minin community during the last miners' strike. This wes a true story involvin my Gran Kay's neebours in Goston's Manse Close, the McSkimmings. Here's hou auld Matha Morton tells the story in the play tae a young miner, Chalkie. Chalkie hes juist gien a stound tae Matha's ideals when he reveals that monie o the local miners hes gien up an is gaun back tae wark efter tholin the strike for nearhaund a year.

Chalkie: The haill o Scotland uised tae be solid NUM, Mr Morton, I'm ashamed for us . . . everybody's oot for whit he can get noo.

Matha: God, I mind in the '26, comin back frae Ayr efter visitin ma brither Jimmy – he had a job doon there. He had gien me a present o a coat, an tried tae mak me accept a pound. I kennt he was juist makin ends meet wi his young family, sae I refused. It wes on the bus hame I discovered he had slipped the pound intae ma coat pocket. Ken whit I did wi that pound son . . . I gaed tae the Tally's an bocht eichty thrupenny fish suppers, wan for every man, woman and wean in the Manse Raw. I felt like Santie Claus.

Yer hame wes yer hame toun, yer hame was the fowk there, yer hame wes yer community, yer community wes yer support. Gin I hadnae been brocht up in a lovin hame thirled tae a distinctive community, I wad never hae creatit ocht o value – for aw my wark sinsyne hes howkit oot the gowden seam kythed tae me by ma hame backgrund.

Me . . . hame. I cannae imagine the twa bein sindered ane fae the ither. I hae been lucky, an ma faimily hes been lucky. Hamelessness hes aye been whit happenned tae ither fowk, their hame taen awa, their life shattered, their hopes smoored.

Hameless, bairnless, thowless, fushionless, emptiness. Dreich words tuim o hope.

Hame, bield, shelter . . . gleg words thrang wi hope.

Luck shouldnae come intae it, hope shouldnae come intae it – yer bield, yer shelter, yer hame should be ane o yer inalienable human richts. We Scots ar unco proud o the rampant egalitarianism that distinguishes oor culture. Oor makaris hes aye brocht it tae the fore an gart us tak tent o it. Burns gied us it in thir words:

Then let us pray that come it may,
(As come it will for aw that)
That Sense and Worth o'er a' the earth
Shall bear the gree an' a' that!
For a' that, an a' that,
It's comin yet for a' that,
That man to man the world o'er,
Shall brithers be for a' that

Hamish Henderson brocht the thocht up tae date:

O come all ye at hame wi freedom,
Never heed whit the hoodies croak for doom;
In your hoose a' the bairns o' Adam
Can find breid, barley bree an paintit room.
When Maclean meets wi's freens in Springburn
A' the roses an geans will turn tae bloom,
And a black boy frae yont Nyanga
Dings the fell gallows o' the burghers doon.

As a people, we hae tae mak siccar that thir kinna ideals is aye at the core o Scottish society, despite the chippin awa o the ideals we hae witnessed in the Thatcherite 1980s. We hae resistit her, an we sall mak siccar that the Scottish Parliament whan it comes will hae oor radical speerit engrained in it. For even afore we hae the keys o the Parliament, we hae gaun faurer in this maitter than nearhaund aw the Bills o Richt that hae been creatit. Already scrievit in the Bill o Richts for Scotland that will be pairt o oor Constitution is the statement: 'Ilka bodie sall hae the richt tae shelter'. A hame, as the richt o awbody. That is whit real democracy is aboot . . . an it's comin yet for aw that.

Hamelessness dings doun our dignity – man, woman an wean
Whan freedom comes it maun ne'er be seen in Scotland again!

Madainn Diardaoin, Ann an Oifis Puist an Glaschu

RUARAIDH MACTHÒMAIS

Bho shràidean
agus bho chaol-shràidean a' bhaile
chruinnich iad
gu Oifis a' Phuist,
na bacaich agus na ciorramaich:
fear a' slaodadh nan casan càm aige,
duin' òg le sgreaban dubh' air aodann,
fear eile le na sùilean ag at 'na cheann,
boireannach letheach-òg
creachte leis an òl,
seann bhodach 'na shliopairean,
bun-feusaig is falt fada,
is briogais thana,
gach duine 's a shùil air toiseach a' chiudha
's a bhileag 'na làimh,
a' dol gu fuaran an fhàsaich
far a robh a' chuirm,
dall is mar a bhà iad
a' leantainn an t-solais,
bodhar is cluais ri ceòl.
Sheall mi gun fhios nach robh Crìosda
air cùl a' chunntair,
ach bha na bacaich ann a sin cuideachd.
Mise 'nam sheasamh anns a' chiudha
a' smaoineachadh gu robh mi slàn.

Thursday Morning, in a Glasgow Post Office

DERICK THOMSON

From the streets
and from the back-streets of the city
they converged
on the Post Office,
the lame and the halt:
a man dragging his crooked legs along,
a young man with black scars on his face,
another whose eyes bulged from his head,
a youngish woman
haggard with drink,
an old man in his slippers,
stubbly beard and long hair,
wearing thin trousers,
each one looking to the head of the queue,
holding his slip of paper,
going to the spring in the desert
where the feast was,
blind and following the light,
deaf and eager for music.
I looked to see if Christ
was behind the counter,
but the halt were there too.
Standing in the queue there
thinking I was whole.

A Sheltered Memory

I. M. Julian Reeves

HAYDEN MURPHY

PROLOGUE: SNAKE SLOW WAS THE SPIT

I was,
And indeed I am, afraid of failure.
Whether it be the inability to hold a drink,
A conversation, a woman or a man, close enough
To my mind to absorb and embrace them entirely.

I went
To the zoo to commune with a snake
I had seen on the news. On a blurred television
In a silent pub where the barman waved goodbye.
I was encouraged by fate. It was a Sunday.
Anniversary of illegal entombments
Of lonely people all over the world.

I sat
With you for an hour, snake, and only saw
Helplessness. A spit at the glass.
A spit at your reflection. I wanted to spit
Back. To tell you, you were not alone. But I was afraid
It might rebound. Become a personal assault.
And, as you and I know, suicide is dangerous.

I sat.
Children threw nuts through cages.
Parents threw dubious glances at me.
You greedily opened a butterfly pattern behind glass.
It was difficult to tell anything from your eyes.

Yet
When you died a week later
I was sure that you were aware.
That you were awake. It was I was elsewhere.
Otherwise why should I feel your spit in my mouth?

MNEMONICS FOR AN IMAGINATION: Part IV

On the day J's body was found in the outhouse of Sonia's maisonette a snake in a glass cage expired in Belfast Zoo. The body was half eaten away. The remains of the corpse were fed to the wolves. In London, after an autopsy, J was cremated.

Trinity College, Dublin, was a sheltered place in September 1965. Catholics were welcomed but permitted to enter only if protected by Priests' and Bishops' dispensation. H resented this. Difference was not yet a virtue.

The Fabian Society attracted all the faithful. Aspiring Communists, lapsed Catholics and the neo-colonial members of the Arts Faculty from England and elsewhere. J was different. He was a devout and practising Catholic, a preaching Maoist, a medical student. He carried a baby, was unmarried and was mature. Indeed he was a mature student. Fifteen years older then the eldest teenager. His background was vague. The baby a vociferous, unmothered she. Three days a week she monopolised at least one babysitting Fabian. J was a part-time but active Samaritan.

Housing in Dublin caused dissent. Georgian squares were being emptied. Suburbs were becoming squats for impersonal towers. Corporation Estates made mud of the green belts. And then there were the Travellers. Itinerants, tinkers, beggars, called whatever the vindictive chose. They were not so much a lost people as a battalion of lost causes.
    J organised a lorry outside the gates of Trinity College. Fabians and a photographer piled in. Less ostentatiously trade unionists, Republicans and students from UCD (the national university) and the Arts College joined them on an acre site on the fringe of the city. Cherry Orchard it was called. Neither trees nor fruit were ever in sight.

Twenty caravans were served by one recently installed tap. Gas fires fumed beneath paraffin lamps. Basic survival was the modest proposal. Literacy and numeracy were aimed at by the incoming 'teachers'.

Mocking alphabets were explicated. A to C, or D until a name could be scribed, a form filled. J worked in close liaison with Gratten, the live-in teacher, the self-elected leader, the self-designated voice of the people. 'The Travelling People'. J and Gratten were English. Well-meaning. But English. Outsiders were not always different enough to be accepted merely as strange.

Gratten's woman was Irish, with an acquired English accent. She was also one-legged. Daily she strapped on her left leg. The bare stump intrigued the youngsters in her classes. 'We shall overcome,' they sang and viewed the curve that was her artificial limb. It would lend class to the begging position. They collectively lusted. Outside the camp a police car parked. Watching. Waiting.

In the late 1960s the Samaritans came out from behind their phones. A soup-kitchen was set up and called, with due deference to history, A Shelter. Needle-thin people came near for warmth and swapped bottles, needles, gossip and prescriptions. H was sick with fear. J was enviously calm. 'It's not the needle, it's the vein that hurts the eye.' He held the shakers. Listened to the sweat break into speech.

When Diogenes was discovered begging money from a statue he explained that he was practising disappointment.

News of the evictions came through sympathetic columnists in *The Irish Times*. 'A Clean Out' had been called for. Later that night the Travellers decided to move. Their own choice. Gratten used words like 'of their own volition' to the cameras. He objected to their decision. He wanted 'positive opposition to the bureaucrats'. He was outspoken, outvoted and dismissed by the fourteen families involved. He then spoke of 'disenchantment' to a convenient microphone. 'Yellow-bellies' is never an acceptable term to the vulnerable, the terrified, the dispossessed.

At dawn police cars, water-control engineers and demonstrators arrived. Ten of the caravans had gone. The site was quiet. All the children had been removed. No one noticed the smoke at first. The first flame was a shock. The subsequent scream a cry of despair. The police, unsure of what was happening, moved to keep the demonstrators from entering the field. The orchard, the once cherried orchard, was barren again, was way beyond ever bearing fruit again.

It became obvious that the caravan on fire was that of the 'Outsiders'. 'Them'. Another scream was one of anger rather than pain. A figure was dumped and rolled on the dew-wet grass. She remained prone, purple with indignation. Gratten was telling the microphone that he had called the fire brigade. She called him a liar from the mud. The fancy-dressed saviours who arrived two hours later were unable to connect to a water supply. It had been cut off the night before. Before the anonymous call to *The Irish Times*.

The screams from the surrounds of the flaming caravan had stopped being fierce. They were now fearful. There was a splutter of cylinders, a series of mild explosions and then the lights went out. All was dead dark with smoke. Shrill with renewed screams.

Years later H asked J how he had got inside the police cordon. How had he been near that particular caravan. 'No matter,' he said. And H by then had learned enough not to ask more.

But out of the smoke, flame-lit, had come J swinging by its leather tongs a silver gleaming amputated leg-stump.

'Good for begging purposes,' one of the youngsters had said, learning how to speak grand.

There was no noise as this odd Englishman buckled it on to the now quiet woman. He held the smoke-smothered figure close to himself, and breached a barricade from the other side.

Blind Borges held on to the hand attached to the voice murmuring how honoured 'we' were to meet him. 'Isn't everybody?' he said in a disappointed tone.

In London J was in controlled shock. He missed the latest baby but felt he had been too often a father to be a parent. His 'patch' was a curiously genteel area near the British Museum. A square acre of dwellers encompassed by a shock of expensive clubs and pubs. It was five years since H had seen him. The smoking had stopped. Des Wilson was aged by a stoop, earnest with youth, but curiously calming. J was not. He shook as he poured tea from a most unhygienic-looking kettle. H saw only eyes beyond the perspiration and the insulating cabin-hut grille.

Later they did the rounds of the hostels. Twenty beds were salvation for the abandoned and the abandoning. Back on the streets were the rejected and the despairing. Grim-faced, J moved towards a figure. The conversation was brief, the directions succinct.

In single file three figures crossed the road and pointed to another figure crouched underneath a triangle of abandoned underground sewer pipes. J went ahead. The knife had cut his coat before he could move away. He talked, and talked. The voice was even. The matured sadness drowned the desperation. Blood was starting to stain the bag handcuffed to his wrist. He was now a qualified doctor with an open-wound locum, carrying drugs for the demented and the desolate. Three hours later. Twenty-two stitches later, Tim, the knifer, the would-be killer, was asleep. J was shaking towards another insomniac night. The blood being transfused into his arm was only restoring an element of life.

Days later H and J went to a poetry reading. Words became sounds. They held hands, often to a curious policeman's annoyance. 'Queers,' he said and they felt queer attracting such belligerence. There was a meal, a pint, an embrace, a farewell. J was being picked up by the soup-van at midnight. H was going to Edinburgh for the Festival.

Ann was graceful. 'Gazelle', H called her in his middle-mind. She was the first to know of the body found in the maisonette. She was the second to know that J had wanted to take his own way out of our lives.

Sonia had killed herself three days earlier. 'Self-inflicted depression', said some. J had eased her off the needle, heroin, two years earlier.

For some three years after his death letters arrived to H from all over Europe. J had requested that they be posted by his hosts, his many friends if anything and everything stopped for him. They were nearly all dated five years earlier. Two years after he had qualified as a doctor. A year later he had become a qualified psychiatrist with an MA in English. His thesis was on Jonathan Swift. *A Modest Proposal.* All this was one year before he left Dublin to join Shelter in 'The City of Dreadful Nights'. The letters were postscripts for some. J being dead meant a part of H stopped living.

McDaid's Bar, Harry Street, Dublin, was full. The 'Orphans' from Lower Mount Street were celebrating. *Dr Strangely Strange*, their in-house pop-group, had made a minor hit for somebody's till. H had his second book of poems on the table. Pat was to marry Tim. Paddy O'Brien, behind the bar, was beaming. A convenient, convivial 'slate' was in motion.

In Belfast a bomb blast upset the equilibrium of a snake. It began to gnaw away at the end furthest from its damaged mind.

In Norwich J was writing 'Killing myself may be worse than dying, but I cannot stand being helpless any more'.

A week later hungry wolves were fed and the remains of a friend cremated.

EPILOGUE: THE DEATH IS REGISTERED

We have tried to transfer, with muted skill, your death
Into complex memories of your life. We rehearsed grief
As a juggler his tricks and found in our self-conscious
Artistry that it was your life in the air between our hands.

Inside this pattern you could have been a dying child.
With you innocent awareness of pain was something
Like shame, to be cured or avoided. We were pin-pointing
Complexity. The butterfly that is idealised piety.

We realised the idea of escape was real
When we joined a nervous system to the sense of loss.
With the ignorance of selfishness we pedestalled our pride,
Aware only of our isolation from sensation.

We registered your absence,
Not as a person seen on a yesterday,
But as a gap in conversation filled by silence.

You are dead. The death is registered.
A moment to be recollected at another date.
In hostile impotence we write you away with an epitaph.

You left us a memory of calm
Cavorting around our interests. The will was read
By each of us in private. We are all left the same

Immovable kindness. Your gentleness and love
Are tender, raw nerves in the present. Memories.
We are sheltered tenants given a home by your friendship.

Auld Wife's Tale

KATHLEEN JAMIE

I says, Oh. Do you ken
it wiz six year past it's no
lang in passin but it's no
that yin, ken, it's th'ither yin's
gaun
      kinna
            mottlt
like when ye sit ower lang at the fire . . .
it's creepin ower,
this
          mottlin,

so I sayed Nithin
tae the Doctur, but whit I dinnae unerstaun:
it isnae the briest that hid the treatment
if it wiz
          I could understaun
if it wiz
          I could weir it.
The morn's morn an it starts wi an Em
this thing they're gonna dae I dinnae ken
the name o't yer mither kens, she wid, she says:

'Thir'll be nae pain they jist hittae clamp yer briest'
Clamp yer briest! Twa buses. I'll hittae
be oot the hoose at skreich o dawn
he says THERE'S NOTHING TO WORRY ABOUT MRS CAMPBELL
IT'S JUST A DELAYED REACTION TO THE RADIOTHERAPY.

But I do worry, hen.

The Interview

MARY GLADSTONE

For her interview Elizabeth decided to buy herself a new pair of tights. She found a pair in Safeway's for fifty-five pence in the right colour. As she rummaged through the packets she made up her mind not to get fifteen denier because they'd inevitably catch on her stripped pine chairs and then ladder. She realised that twenty denier was the right thickness.

She was pleased she had avoided the alcohol section; a cheap Riesling would have been fine even though it might have anti-freeze in it. Maybe that's what she needed to thaw her out, but today she felt anything but frozen. In fact, she could feel herself sweating freely. Remembering her friend Jennifer's advice to take deep breaths and be positive, she tried to think well of herself as she wheeled her trolley along the aisles. But it was easy for Jennifer with all that money. On £36.70 a week, though, it's hard always to be positive.

A tall, emaciated woman of about sixty walked past her. The figure had the look of someone who was sick, someone even who might be dying, Elizabeth thought, with eyes that were dewy but with none of the clarity you find in the gaze of youth. *Her* look was more akin to resignation – a resignation to The Final Act with no hope of a *deus ex machina* flying down from the gods. Elizabeth yanked her trolley to the left to avoid collision with the woman.

When she reached the check-out, the assistant tried to charge her ninety pence for mushrooms that were only thirty. A moment of panic; to find that sixty pence wouldn't be there at the end of the day, when she had successfully avoided drinking a half-pint in a bar, was too much for her, especially when she had eschewed a coffee at Tranent's, and even stopped herself from indulging in buying a book. How she had wanted it! The biography of Gwen John. The woman who had effaced herself so much that she'd found salvation through her very self-neglect. In other words, thought Elizabeth, she had lost her life in order to save it.

Casting a last look at the alcohol section, she considered again the

Riesling she'd seen for just under two pounds. She *could* have bought a bottle. She remembered the time not long ago when she'd buy one bottle almost every night from the Asian shop where the two brothers knew her as 'the woman with the wine'. To think of it, she mused, to be not the woman with the lamp, but with the wine! She laughed at herself and was pleased she could do that still.

A part of her identified with these Asians because she shared with them that feeling of not totally belonging. Her father had come over here from Poland during the war. She knew well why they tried so hard to fit in.

Anyway, she wouldn't think of the Asians – nor of the wine. Not at the moment anyhow, because it was the interview she was to consider. With the tights and her good coat and her shoes that were all right, she'd go up there to the top of the town quite confidently. Or would she? She wasn't so sure. Two years out of work. Two years!

What had she done to be out of work for two years? Of course, she wouldn't tell him the *real* reason. She couldn't reveal why she'd hardly stepped out of her front door for six months of those two years, how she'd lived like a hermit speaking to no one except perhaps to the woman in the greengrocer's, the Asians and the Polish shoemaker off St Denzil's Street. Perhaps it was because her father was a Pole that she was drawn to the shoemaker. He was always friendly and would rail against those who lived off 'the Social Security'. Elizabeth hadn't the courage to admit that *she* was one of those people.

When she went to the Post Office every fortnight to cash her Giro-cheque, she couldn't help feeling ashamed. On the one hand, she knew that her father – dead now for over two and a half years – wouldn't have liked to see her living off the government. *He'd* never begged or borrowed money – not even from his family and times had been hard when he was young. 'But not as hard as it was for those left behind,' he would often say, and then launch into the tale of the brother who'd been in the Resistance and ended up in Dachau. Elizabeth didn't want to think of the uncle in Dachau nor of her father who had died, not suddenly, but in a hospice close to the sea on the outskirts of the city. She shuddered at the memory.

It was raining outside. A lorry hurtled by, sending up a spray of water that splashed her legs. If it continued to rain when she walked up the hill for her appointment, she would look a mess when she arrived. Umbrellas in this weather with a prevailing cruel Forth wind provided little protection. Pausing at the traffic lights by the off-licence, she noticed the tall woman she'd seen in the supermarket, walking on the other side of the street, pushing a shopping-basket on wheels. Her step was light, though she had a trace of a limp. Even from a distance it was noticeable that she was suspended from this sphere, removed from it, by what seemed a terminal pain.

Elizabeth took a considerable length of time unwrapping the tights. 'Some people wear gloves so they don't ladder their stockings when they put them on,' her mother once told her. Elizabeth would visit her occasionally, just enough to salve her conscience. She knew she should go more often, but if she did, she might undo the good of going at all by arguing with her mother. Pretending that she agreed with her was too much of a strain, so Elizabeth went little.

'Lipstick?' she asked herself. Why not? A little blue on the lids? Her mother always put on too much make-up. Far too much, but then, her mother hadn't come to terms with ageing. She was almost seventy and she *still* couldn't let a grey hair stay on her head for more than a couple of days; and her little-girl voice that might have disarmed her father forty years ago, fooled no one today.

The door was large and imposing and she had arrived five minutes too early. No time for a coffee opposite. She walked up the stairs that were carpeted in a hairy material and noticed the colourful posters on the walls. She asked to see the director, who she said was expecting her. A receptionist (ash-blonde and as slim as Elizabeth had always longed to be) told her to sit outside in the passageway and wait for him.

He arrived. 'Would you come this way, please?' he said.

She knew he was formal in a way that wasn't natural. She knew he wasn't *her* cup of tea. She knew she wanted to walk briskly out of his office down those hairy carpeted stairs back into the street. But she knew she wouldn't. She watched the long, thin man peruse her form. How do you hide two years of life that were, in effect, spent in hiding? How do you assume that confident, inside manner when you know only too well that if you don't get some kind of job soon, you'll slip inexorably outside this world that they call the world of the living?

The man wasted no time in coming to the point. 'I see,' he mumbled in a manner that reminded her of a judge preparing to pronounce a sentence on the defendant (defendant she certainly felt, defending her very life but with little effect), 'from your CV that you have a gap of . . . let's see,' he squinted through his spectacles at the paper on his desk, 'two years.' He sat back and looked at her carefully. She knew she must explain why she had had two years out, and tried to fool him that she was relaxed by swinging her right leg over the knee of her left, leaning deliberately back in her chair. 'I decided I wanted to take time out to . . .'

She couldn't finish her sentence. What could she say when the reason would condemn her completely? 'I suppose you could call it a sabbatical,' she said eventually.

The man looked at her sceptically. 'Two years?' he asked incredulously. By some form of miracle or flash of inspiration, she found herself making up a story about why she'd not worked for so long and said, 'I thought I would try my hand at becoming a . . .' (she wasn't sure why she hesitated yet again) '. . . a painter.' She murmured something about self-expression and wanting to 'know herself'.

'I never sold anything,' she added for precaution, 'but I got a few favourable comments on my . . . watercolours.' She began to like her story and only wished that she remembered to say gouaches instead of watercolours, then realised she might have been sailing a little close to the wind when she had no idea what gouaches were.

'Most irregular, I'd have thought, to give up the promising career that you had,' was the response.

He asked another question, and then several more until she found herself feeling not unlike an onion being peeled right down to its core – that's if onions had cores. He wanted to be sure she was reliable, he said, that's why he was grilling her. After all, after two years of being out of the system she might not be able to teach. She had to convince him of her stamina, reliability and adequacy.

How could she show him she was now more adequate than she'd been before? Anyone who had been through what she'd been through and emerged intact had more than enough ability to do what this man required of her. Elizabeth began to wonder if she wanted to be part of his establishment anyway. The money would be pleasant, but money wasn't the only thing she wanted and there was always £36.70 for her to subsist on each week, plus sunshine and walks in the Botanics. Never mind about buying books about Gwen John. She would *be* Gwen John, she thought, with wild bravura, then quickly came back to earth, realising she had the talent neither for painting nor for poverty.

The man's face was cold and disinterested. Elizabeth couldn't be bothered to try and win him round – to seduce him with fluttering eyelids, hunched shoulders and coy smiles.

'Well, Miss Tadeuska, thank you very much for coming in,' he said briskly. 'I *have* enjoyed talking with you. If we need any extra help this summer, we'll let you know.'

She found herself standing outside the door on the hairy carpet. She walked quickly down the steps and didn't care where she went so long as she could be in the street without being noticed. There was a comfort in being unknown.

She followed a party of Japanese sightseers all gazing up at the castle in a uniform expression. She carried on walking down to Tranent's for a coffee; what the hell, she could afford it this once! Lounging in that cavernous room with the gentle background hiss of the coffee-machine intermingling with the douce whispers of women taking a break from their afternoon's shopping, Elizabeth noticed that by listening in to their chatter, she could live vicariously for a while; this was compensation for her own lack of engagement with the world. Elizabeth wiped her mouth with a red paper serviette, stood up from the table, and straightened her grey flannel skirt. As she climbed up the steps to the pavement, she was surprised to see again the woman she had almost bumped into earlier in the day in Safeway's. She was looking in the window of the florist's next to the coffee-house, where displayed in all their splendour was a bouquet of gardenias, with a dozen lilies and roses. She paused momentarily, gazing up at the window, then quickly moved on down the street towards the West End.

It must have been the effect of the interview that did it; the layers that had been exposed couldn't immediately be restored to their original position. Elizabeth was impelled to walk up the steps and go into the shop to ask the assistant if she could buy the bouquet. What was more, she didn't even ask the price, which turned out to be all of eighteen pounds, more than half her weekly allowance. Quickly paying for them, she ran out of the shop with the flowers and followed the woman, whose presence had dogged her all day.

Catching up with her, Elizabeth tapped her on the shoulder. The woman turned round and looked her straight in the eye. Noticing that her expression had the authority and lack of temerity only found in those resigned to their fate, Elizabeth was certain the woman was dying. She'd seen that look so clearly once before, back in the hospice two and a half years before, when her father lay there waiting for death. Elizabeth held out the bouquet to the woman, who scrutinised her closely. Without a word, she accepted the flowers, whispering her thanks afterwards. With a detached regality, she departed down the street.

As soon as she returned home, Elizabeth removed her tights, not with gloves as her mother had once advised, and soaked them in warm water in the wash-hand basin. After making herself a cup of coffee, she sat down in her armchair, and thought about her day. It had been just another day, nothing more and nothing less.

Bedfordshire

DOUGLAS DUNN

Have you noticed the dunderheids toddling our streets
With their furtive manoeuvres, yawns, grunts and bleats,
Slouching, and shuffling, at dead slow and plod,
Somniferous, jaded disciples of Nod?

'We'd be much better off in our beds,' they all say
In a chorus that sounds like a half-swallowed yawn
Crossed with sighs of deep puzzlement, fear and dismay,
As they dawdle and mumble and look put-upon.

There's Alice, there's Alec. – They were once very busy
Devoted to causes and not good at quitting;
But the forty-first wink's undone Alice's tizzy
While Alec's old tantrums are coddled by knitting.

'Lethargy's dormice, that's what we've chosen to be.
We're out on a supine and intimate strike.
Pass me my slippers. Pour my mandragora tea.
Inertia's lovely, and slumbering *is* what we like.'

'We happen to think that our sullen siesta's
Richly deserved, and no more than what we are due.
Damn all animation, and damn all fiestas!
'Night-'night! And, really, it ought to be bye-byes for *you*.'

'The ones with velocity, business, and thrust,
Lickspittle factotums of main enterprise,
Insomniac creatures, we'll water their fidgety dust,
Then sprinkle our Morphean sand in their eyes.'

'Our country's in coma in mischievous Dreamland, ho-hum.
Torpor-led voters have chosen stagnation's
Laid-back annoyance, the gesture of sucking the thumb.
Instead of two-fingers, we give you our back-turned orations.'

'Hymn me the downy, the duvet and eiderdown,
Orthopedic four-poster, the big feather-bed,
Lyrical jim-jams and red-flannel ankle-length gown,
Significant snoozes, narcosis, the ploys of the dead.'

'Please switch off the light. Disengage and resign.
We'll soon reach the peak of the old wooden hill.
We're reclining, defeated; we're in a decline,
Resisting what happens with naughtily negative will.'

Then they puffed up their pillows and planted their heads,
Dead to the world in their negligent beds.
Oppositional snores won't correct what is wrong,
Nor slumbering satire, nor wry cradlesong.

A' Ghort Mhór

SOMHAIRLE MACGILL-EAIN

(I)

Neòil na gorta le samh sgreataidh
Ann an deàrrsadh na gréine,
A' seargadh feòil air cnamhan,
A' deanadh culaidh-ghràin de bhoidhche.
Cìochan a bha daingeann corrach
'Nan ropan an crochadh ri cléibh,
Sléisdean is calpannan a bha cuimir
'Nam biorain chrìona connaidh,
'S a' bhru a bha cho sliom seang
'na bolla tioram teann oillteil.

(II)

'S ioma gort is tart mhór
A bh' air an t-saoghal o thùs,
Gun telebhis gan craoladh
Gu na bailtean reamhar saoibhir,
Gun ghuth réidio gan innse
Do chluasan coibhneil no coma,
'S do chluasan teth le nàire,
'Do chluasan nan naomh 's nan aingidh,
'S do chluasan a bha 'g éisdeachd
Ri acras an cloinne fhéin.

(III)

'Ne 'm peacadh a rinn an sgrios seo,
An sgrios fada fichead uair as motha
Na teine 's prunnasdan nam frasan
A dhòirt air Bailtean na Machrach?
Bheil nàdur coma co-dhiù
'S an Taghadh fuar-chridheach borb?

The Great Famine

SORLEY MACLEAN

(I)

The clouds of famine with loathsome stink
in the glitter of the sunlight,
withering flesh on bones,
making beauty a disgusting thing.
Breasts that were firm, upstanding,
ropes hanging to rib cages,
thighs and calves that were shapely
brittle sticks of fire-wood,
and the belly that was sleek and slender
a dry tight hideous buoy.

(II)

Many a famine and great thirst
were in the world from the start
without television broadcasting them
to the fat wealthy towns,
with no radio voice telling them
to kindly or uncaring ears,
and to ears hot with shame,
to the ears of saints and of the wicked,
and to the ears that were listening
to the hunger of their own children.

(III)

Was it sin that made this destruction,
a destruction far more than twenty times greater
than the fire and brimstone of the showers
that poured on the Cities of the Plain?
Does Nature not care at all
and is the Predestination cold-hearted and cruel?

(IV)

Còrr is fichead muillion,
Barrachd, barrachd ioma h-uair
Na bhàsaich ann an Gort na h-Eireann,
Còrr is fichead muillion,
Co a thomhaiseas an cràdh
An ciùrradh a shracas an cridhe
Ged nach robh ann ach a h-aon,
Aon leanabh air nach fhacas
Blath iongantach na h-òige,
Am blàth a dh'fhaodadh mairsinn
Ioma bliadhna gun sheargadh,
Ròsan a' fosgladh gu làn àilleachd.

(V)

Cridheachan màthar is athar,
agus peathar is bràthar
Riabte leis na tàirnean meirgeach,
Le spealgan iarainn nan sligean
A thig gun sian as an adhar
A dh'innse mu chor an t-saoghail.

(VI)

Có as a thug sibh a' choiseachd
'Nur triuir chompanach an-iochdmhor,
A' ghort 's an laige 's an calar?
Co as a thàinig sibh le 'r sgreamh,
Co as a thàinig sibh idir?
'N ann as an aineolas rag,
No as a' pheacadh mhór,
As a' pheacadh bheag,
No as a' pheacadh mhor,
No as an fhéinealachd choma,
No as an aingidheachd fhéin
No as a' ghamhlas as miosa,
Is mac an duine cho coir
Cho iochdmhor coibhneil laghach,
Cho cùramach mu chor a' chloinne?

(IV)

More than twenty million,
more, more many a time
than died in the Famine of Ireland,
more than twenty million,
who will measure the pain,
the torture that tears the heart
though there was only one
one child on whom there was not seen
the wonderful bloom of youth,
the bloom that might last
many a year without fading,
ropes opening to full beauty.

(V)

Hearts of mother and father
and of sister and brother
torn with the rusty nails,
with iron splinters from shells
that come without whizz from the sky
to tell of the world's plight.

(VI)

From where have you walked,
you three merciless companions,
famine, weakness and cholera?
From where have you come with your loathsomeness.
From where have you come at all?
Is it from stubborn ignorance
or from the uncaring laziness,
from the small sin,
or from the great sin,
or from the indifferent selfishness
or from wickedness itself
or from the worst malice,
though mankind is so generous,
so merciful, kind and pleasant,
so careful of the state of his children.

(VII)
Tha 'n Afraic fada thall
Ach tha 'n telebhis faisg
Air rumannan comhfhurtail
'S air bùird beairteach le biadh
Is deoch is airgead dearrsach
'S gach sochair eile th' aig an stamag
'S aig an t-suil 's aig a' bhlas
Agus aig miannan na colainn.

(VIII)
Ciamar a roinnear am biadh?
Ciamar a dh'uisgeachar an fhàsach?
Bheil bàs na gorta 's a chalair
Do-sheachanta mar a bha
Fad gach ginealach a thàinig,
Fad gach ginealach a thig?

(IX)
Am faigh gach fear is bean is nighean
Is mac is leanaban a mhillear
Agus a mharbhar le gort is calar
Pàrras shìorruidh an spioraid
Fad àlan buan na biothbhuantachd?
Bu mhath am prionnsapal 's an riadh
A bhiodh 'nan éirig air na thachair,
An eirig a dh'fheumadh na miltean
'S na ciadan muillion de chreutairean
An déidh anacothrom na beatha.

(VII)

Africa is far away
but television is near
comfortable rooms
and near tables rich with food
and drink and gleaming silver
and every other privilege of the stomach
of the eye and the taste
and the desires of the body.

(VIII)

How will food be shared?
How will the desert be watered?
Is death from famine and cholera
unavoidable as was
throughout every generation that has come,
throughout every generation that will come?

(IX)

Will every man and woman and daughter
and son and infant that will be spoilt
and killed with famine and cholera,
will all of them get the eternal Paradise of the spirit
through the lasting generation of infinity?
How good would the principal and interest be
as ransoms needed by the thousands
and hundreds of millions of creatures
after the great distress of life.

A Good Night's Sleep
BRIAN MCCABE

Just when he was maybe beginning to fall asleep at last, George Lockhart, an insomniac, thought he heard something bumping softly against his door. He opened his eyes to the darkness and listened. There it was again, against the door of his flat, soft but insistent.

He tried to rearrange himself more comfortably in the bed and sighed a sleepless curse. The noise had been getting to him lately. All the noises from the street below. Lockhart lived on the third floor of a tenement building in Edinburgh and although the street he lived in wasn't one of the busiest, there were always these noises puncturing the quiet – squeals of taxi-brakes, car doors being slammed, the musak from the late-night bar downstairs. When the bar closed, a few of its customers usually stood around on the pavement outside, gabbling loudly. Once they'd said their repetitive goodnights, there was usually a lull and sometimes he managed to get to sleep before the Chinese restaurant closed up. The staff always seemed to be having a heated controversy as they set the alarm, locked up, ignited their engines and roared off to the casino. Often too there were bands of students being extrovert on the way home from their pubs and their parties, and more than once that inflated laughter had set him thinking about his own student days, the flats he'd lived in then, the parties he'd gone to, the girls he'd gone out with . . . set him thinking, and so kept him awake. Worse were the tribes of drunks, branding the night with their threats, their slogans and their chants. And then there were the miscellaneous voices of the night – the garbled, gruesome shouts of the forsaken and the damned.

Something bumping softly against his door.

Sometimes there were noises from the building itself as well as the noises from the street. The old guy with the limp who lived upstairs. He was always coming home wildly drunk, and Lockhart would have to listen to his demented monologue as he heaved himself up the stairs, stopping every few steps to argue with some remembered or imagined enemy. Worse were his bouts of song. Amplified and distorted by the stairwell, they sounded like the wails of a wounded, cornered animal. And, of course, there were the people through the wall, the new people who'd moved in recently and who were always having rows. They'd had one of their disputes tonight, complete with slamming doors and breaking glass. A strained silence, then the muted duet of argument that meant they were over the worst of it. After a while, he'd heard them going out. He was anxious to be unconscious before they came home and started kicking their shoes off, playing their blues records and making it up in bed – their good times could be just as noisy as their bad.

Now this, surely not the wind, in any case not worth paying any attention to.

It was urgent that he fall asleep immediately, because as well as an insomniac Lockhart was a teacher of Communication and General Studies, with the first year first thing in the morning. He'd got them having a series of discussions recently on the Problems of Modern Society. They'd done Pollution. Unemployment. Race Relations. Last week it had been Drugs and tomorrow it was what?

He turned over and tried to concentrate on not thinking about anything, so that maybe he wouldn't and therefore go out like a light – as if sleep could be crept up on from behind and be taken unawares. Of course he knew, from the yawning years of wrestling with his demons, as the dawn light seeped through his curtains, that sleep couldn't be crept up on, couldn't be taken unawares. It had to take you – a bit like orgasm and, as far as Lockhart was concerned, nowadays every bit as longed for. It was months since he'd slept with anybody and now he didn't know which he needed most – the sleep, or the anybody.

He punched the pillow, clenched his teeth, rearranged his legs and his arms. It was one of those expensive beds, scientifically designed for the sleepless, but single when all is said and as such harder than some. He tried not to think of Elaine, his ex-wife, sleeping in their old, comfortable double-bed – alone? – and tried not to start worrying about what to do with Ben, their son, when he took him for the weekend . . .

He heard it again then, against the door of his flat, softly bumping. It wasn't anyone knocking and anyway – why knock? There was a doorbell. And it was too soft to be the old guy with the limp staggering against the door on his way up to his own. This was a different kind of pressure on the door, ceasing and coming again, not making much noise maybe, but enough to keep insomniacs awake. Surely it couldn't be the new people, locked in a passionate embrace against his door, unable to wait until they'd unlocked their own?

He propped himself up on one elbow, switched on the bedside lamp and gave the clock-without-a-tick a dirty look. The time it told wasn't the right time, because Lockhart had developed the habit of setting it ten minutes fast, so that if need be he could take ten minutes longer to surface in the morning – as if time could be stolen from Time. Even so it said 01.45 – the wrong time for a visitor. Maybe it could be that stray cat he'd invited in not so long ago for the remains of a Chinese carry-out – back for its banana fritter? If so, he'd wring its neck.

But no, there it was again, something leaning then not leaning on the door, something bigger than a cat, something heavier and by the sounds of it, less likely to go away.

Tying his dressing-gown on, Lockhart stamped along the chilly hallway in his bare feet, switched on the light and unlocked the door.

– Yes?

The young girl sitting on his doormat looked up sharply as she spat out this affronted 'Yes?', for all the world as if he'd just barged into her bedroom. Maybe he had. He apologised: – I'm sorry, but I heard . . . I wondered what the . . .

– Oh, I'm *so* sorry if I *disturbed* you. I hope I wasn't keeping you *awake!*

Lockhart held the door half-closed and moved from foot to foot in the icy draught, scarcely able to believe that she was there on his doormat, talking to him with such emphatic scorn.

–What are you doing . . . out here?

– I was *trying* to sleep!

– Out *here?*

– What does it look like?

He had to admit that it did. She had spread out an assortment of brightly coloured but tattered clothes on the landing and had bundled others up into what looked like a makeshift pillow.

He watched as she took a pair of lumpy woollen socks from a plastic carrier-bag and tugged them on over her jeans, every so often glaring up at him suspiciously. He went on staring helplessly as she tied on her worn sneakers, taken aback by her presence – by those glowering dark eyes, by the delicate cheekbones and lips. She was young – in her early twenties, maybe younger.

– Don't you have anywhere to *live?*

– I wouldn't be here if I did, would I?

– No . . . I suppose not.

– You suppose right. I'm homeless, that's all. I've been sleeping in stairs for long time now.

– But . . . you're *young!*

– So? A lot of young people are homeless nowadays – haven't you heard?

The teacher of Communication and General Studies hopped around in the icy draught and had to admit that he hadn"t.

– Well you have now. Goodnight. George.

He was startled by her use of his name, then laughed nervously. Of course, it was on the door. She echoed his nervous laugh perfectly, then dropped it suddenly and averted her face.

– But surely there must be somewhere you can go – a hostel, maybe?

– Which hostel is that?

– A hostel, I don't know, for the homeless.

– They don't let me in any more, so I sleep in stairs. Tragic, isn't it? If you know what *tragedy* is.

Lockhart found himself thinking of a grey-haired king wandering around in the homeless wilderness of a first-year literature option, the Fool at his side, but the doorstep at two in the morning was no place for a tutorial.

– Are you a student?

– What's it to you? You a teacher?

Lockhart nodded. The girl stopped blowing into her hands to laugh derisively.

– I might've known it. You look like the sadistic type.

Lockhart ignored this. — Where were you living before?

– Before what?

– Before you weren't.

– Listen, teacher, listen carefully. I had to leave the place I was in. Now I don't have anywhere else to go, so I'm homeless. Got it? Sleep well.

– But that's terrible!

– No it's not. I'll die, that's all. I'll die and I don't care anyway and don't start telling me you do because you fucking well don't, nobody does.

She glared up at him as she spat out the words. Lockhart stood there holding the door and saying nothing. What was there to say to a young girl who was going to die on your doormat at two in the morning?

– You wouldn't have a *cigarette?* Oh, I don't suppose you *smoke* though, do you?

Lockhart replied stiffly that he did smoke, told her to wait a minute, then let the door swing closed on her. He could lock it now, go back to bed, forget her, get a good night's sleep yet if he dropped off right away. After all – why should he have to bother with her? Why did he feel obliged to try and do something to alleviate her plight? Maybe it was the way she sneered as she spoke to him, as if he personally was somehow to blame for her situation.

Back in the warmth of his bedroom, Lockhart lit a cigarette for himself and donned his socks. He could offer her the boy's room for the night. What harm would it do? Or if she preferred, she could just get some rest on the couch until the morning. Or he could call the police. Wouldn't a cell be better than the cold stone landing of a tenement stair, with a doormat for your mattress?

He yawned his way back out to the door. As he stooped to give her the cigarette and the lighter, he noticed the frayed hole in her old pullover and thought he caught a whiff of something bad – like rancid butter, but worse. As she handed back the lighter she bared her teeth in the parody of a smile and said: – Thank you *so much*. You're *so kind*.

He wasn't used to being the target for such venom and didn't know how to react. He hovered over her in silence, holding the door with one hand and smoking with the other. She looked up at him once, laughed sarcastically and looked away. At length, he came out with it:

– Okay. You can stay the night here. My son isn't here at the moment. You can take his bed.

He was just about to add that it was only for one night, that he had to get up early for work and that he'd want to see her gone in the morning, when she interrupted:

– No way.

– But I'm offering you a place to *sleep*!

The word echoed in the hollow stairwell. She glared at him insolently, over her shoulder, her lips parted slightly as if ready to laugh at him at any moment. Then she flicked her ash on the doormat, looked away and shook her head.

– Come *on!* It's a bed for the night!

– I've heard that one before!

– Oh for christsake, I'm not going to . . . *do* anything!

She glanced at him with blatant accusation, as if to say that because he'd mentioned it, he must have thought about it.

Lockhart groaned with emphasis and waited. He thought she might be hesitating, but it was taking too long and so he told her that he had to sleep, had to get up early and he hoped she'd find a place to stay soon.

As he turned the key in the lock he heard her, on the other side of the door, bid him a quiet goodnight, all hostility gone from her voice, without that sharp edge of scorn.

Lockhart thumped the light-switch with the side of his fist and padded back along the hallway to bed. Turning over and over in the warmth of it, trying not to think about her out there on his doormat, he heard it again, the softly bumping sound as she leaned back against the door. She must be trying to get comfortable, or not comfortable exactly but into a position for sleep. Lockhart endeavoured to do the same. Then he heard her coughing, weakly at first, then it was a harsh, hacking cough that echoed in the stairwell. She was definitely going to die out there and she didn't care – *And don't start telling me you do because you fucking well don't. Nobody does!* – and Lockhart wondered if he'd maybe been too impatient with her. Yet he felt angry too, angry with her arrogance: how dare she not care about herself! Why should he care about her, if *she* didn't? Why should anyone?

Again he heard her cough.

When he could suffer it no longer, he climbed out of bed again and switched on the lamp. Then he heard the voices outside, in the stair. It was the couple next door, the new people. He couldn't make out what they were saying, but the man's voice was raised. His wife's voice was high-pitched, accusing. He thought he heard the young girl – her sneering rejoinder. After a few minutes the voices subsided. Then he heard the key rattling in the lock of the flat next door. He hurried out and unlocked his door in time to catch his neighbours closing theirs. The woman was already inside, but the man stopped on his threshold when he saw Lockhart. There was no sign of the young girl. Lockhart found himself apologising again.

– Sorry. I heard the . . . I wondered what the . . .

– Oh, it was just some junkie sleeping in the stair.

– Really?

– Yeah. I told her where to go.

– Did you? Where?

– Where d'you think?

Lockhart glimpsed his neighbour's tight little smile before the man turned and stepped into his hallway.

– See you.

– Yes, goodnight.

They locked their respective doors.

Lockhart switched off the lamp, then stepped over to the window, parted the curtains and peered down into the dark canyon of the street. He couldn't see her anywhere, but her voice was still there in his head, bidding him a quiet goodnight as he locked the door on her, as if she'd felt able to own up to her helplessness only with the door between them.

He turned from the window but didn't get into bed. What was the hurry? The luminous digits on the clock told him in any case that he'd never get a good night's sleep now. He stood in the darkness of the room, listening to the woman through the wall kicking off her shoes one by one, to the voices resuming their duet, to the music with its thudding bass, the man's laughter and the woman's shrill cry of mock surprise . . . Didn't they have work to go to in the morning, these new people? He had the first year, and another of the many Problems of Modern Society. It had to be homelessness.

He climbed into bed, closed his eyes and immediately began to drift into a deep, deep sleep, then he heard it again, against the door of his flat, soft but insistent.

The Warehouse

AGNES OWENS

The middle-aged couple sat with their backs against the wall while further up on the opposite side some drunks were shouting on them to come over.

'Ignore them. They'll only be wanting some of our drink. Mind you, I thought that fellow with the mouth-organ would have come back this evening. Still, it's early yet.'

'What fellow?' asked the man.

'The one who was in here last Friday. Remember he played some good old-fashioned tunes. There was one I liked in particular. It was kind of Mexican . . .'

'I don't remember.'

'At the time you said you knew it. You were even singing the words.'

'I don't remember,' said the man emphatically. 'What's more important is that this bottle's nearly empty. We'll have to get another.'

The woman pursed her lips. 'There's plenty left. Don't be so desperate –' She broke off when she saw the warehouse door slide open to reveal a young woman standing within the gap. 'Come in and close the door. There's a draught.'

The young woman closed the door behind her then called out that she couldn't see a thing.

'You will in time when you get used to it. How do you think we manage?'

When the young woman finally made her way up to sit beside them explaining that she'd only looked in because she'd heard the voices the older woman said, 'That's all right. It's a free country. So what's your name?'

'Jessica.'

'That's a pretty name.'

Seen close up the woman thought this Jessica looked much more mature than she'd appeared from a distance with her dyed blonde hair and heavily pencilled eyebrows. 'My name's Mavis and this is my friend Albert,' she said, gesturing towards the man who, after a brief glance at the young woman when she came in, had sat with his eyes riveted on the floor.

Mavis offered Jessica the bottle.

'Thanks all the same but I'd rather have a Temazepam or a fag if you've got one to spare.'

'We've no Temazepam but it so happens I've got fags,' said Mavis, bringing out a packet of Embassy Regal from her coat pocket and offering it first to Jessica and then to Albert before taking one herself. After the initial puff she began to cough. 'These fags will be the death of me.'

'Don't get my hopes built up,' said Albert coming to life and winking round at Jessica who gave him a polite smile back.

On noticing this Mavis asked him why he was looking so pleased all of a sudden when he hadn't had a civil word to say all day.

'Me pleased?' he said, surprised. 'What makes you think I'm pleased?'

'Never mind,' she said, becoming downcast for no good reason she could think of, then quickly furious when she saw Jessica had turned her attention towards the drunks on the opposite side of the warehouse and was actually smiling at them. 'Here, don't you be giving them alkies the eye or they'll be over like a shot and we definitely don't want that. At least, I don't.'

'Are you talking to me?' said Jessica, her eyes glittering narrowly.

'Who else?'

Jessica made to rise. 'I'm not stopping to be insulted by the likes of you.'

'Don't then.'

By this time Mavis had taken a strong dislike to the young woman, who, as far as she was concerned, was getting to look more and more like a tart with every minute that passed. She turned to Albert. 'You can see she's only out to cause trouble.'

'Leave her alone and mind your own bloody business,' he said.

Rage boiled up inside her. She lifted the bottle and smashed it against the wall, saturating it with wine, some of it dribbling on to the floor. There was a space of silence during which the three of them stared at the small dark-red puddle.

Finally Albert said, 'There must have been at least a good third left in that bottle,' then he stood up and Mavis thought he was going to strike her. Instead he went over to Jessica and asked if she would like to come outside.

'If you want,' she said, taking a hold of his arm.

Open-mouthed and in a state of shock Mavis watched them leave. By the time she'd pulled herself together and went out after them they had vanished. She hung about for a good while in the hope Albert would regret what he'd done and come back. Perhaps the whole thing had been his idea of a joke or even a punishment for her behaviour. Albert could be very devious on occasions. No one knew better than her how devious, but when time passed without any sign of him she was forced to move away, unsure of everything.

Fifteen minutes later she entered the licensed grocer in order to buy another bottle. It was the only constructive thing she could think of to do, even although she hadn't intended drinking again so soon.

'Your friend, he is not with you this evening?' enquired Abdul who always took a personal interest in the affairs of his customers.

Mavis explained that it appeared he'd left her for another woman.

'But that is terrible. What has came over him?'

She went on to say that it must be because of his age for according to what she'd heard lots of men leave their wives or partners for younger women when they reach a certain time in life: the male menopause it's called, and as the woman he'd gone off with appeared young enough to be his daughter, that's all she could put it down to.

'Perhaps he will regret it later on,' said Abdul, shaking his head in dismay then wrapping up the bottle in brown paper, giving it an extra twist at the top. Mavis always felt like telling him not to bother with the paper as it only got thrown away but she never did in case she hurt his feelings. As she went out the door she promised to let him know of any further developments. Once outside she threw away the paper, unscrewed the top of the bottle and took a long gulp of the wine which immediately put new heart into her to such an extent that she began to see the affair from a different angle. She began to think if Albert never came back she might be better off without him in many ways. She wouldn't have to put up with his foul moods when he had too much to drink. Nor would she have to keep him going in it when she'd hardly enough for herself. Nor would she be obliged to have sex when she didn't feel like it. She hadn't felt like it for years, come to think of it. There were hundreds of things she wouldn't feel obliged to do. Why, life without Albert might not be so bad after all. It was at that point she decided that with her next Giro, instead of spending half of it on him, she would get something decent to wear from the Oxfam then have her hair done, nothing fancy, a cut and blow-dry would do her fine. Then after that, her heart pounding at the very idea of it, she would go to the local housing department and ask for her name to be put down on the list for a council flat. It was time she was getting in off the streets and having a decent life for a change.

As she was walking along the pavement, her head quite dizzy with all these notions of grandeur, she bumped into a woman who told her to watch where she was going and then attempted to push her off the pavement. Mavis's mood quickly changed. 'Who do you think you're shoving?'

'Scum,' said the woman over her shoulder, which made Mavis feel quite depressed although she immediately recognised the truth of the statement, but then if Albert had been with her the situation would never have arisen. Coming to a row of tenement buildings she paused outside one of the entrances wondering whether to have a drink inside rather than risk taking it out in the open, when a young man came out from the building and told her to beat it.

'I was only looking for an address,' she said, as he brushed past her, exuding an air of violence and leaving her dithering on the pavement frightened to move. All her previous confidence vanished. Whatever had made her think she could ever be anything better than she was. The truth of the matter, she told herself sadly, was that on her own she could scarcely walk two steps along the street without somebody picking on her. What a fool she'd been. She'd just have to throw her pride to the wind and go and find Albert. She'd buy him all the drink he needed and he could bring Jessica with him if that's what he wanted. Anything was better than being left on her own. He couldn't be all that far away. She'd try the old warehouse first. He might be there already waiting for her to bring along the bottle.

'Albert,' she called coming into the warehouse and leaving the door open so that she could see her way. There was no answer, but it was still early, perhaps not yet eight o'clock. She had to give him a chance. She reached the spot where they usually sat and took a small sip of wine, at the same time assuring herself she would make this last her until Albert arrived. Otherwise he wouldn't be pleased. To pass the time she smoked three cigarettes one after the other. When she'd finished the third she'd become so jumpy that she put the bottle to her mouth and took a long swig without thinking, then became so befuddled she forgot all about him. The only thing on her mind now was the Mexican tune the man with the mouth-organ had played the previous Friday. The words that had eluded her before came into her head quite easily: 'The mission bells told me, that I must not stray, south of the border, down Mexico way.'

She sang the whole verse and continued to sing it over and over again in a cracked tone of voice. She stopped once when she thought she heard footsteps outside.

'Is that you, Albert?' she called, but when there was no reply she simply carried on singing, enjoying the sound of her own voice and only breaking off now and again to put the bottle to her mouth. She finally stopped altogether when it become so dark that she couldn't see a thing in front of her, which gave her a creepy feeling. She picked up the bottle and discovered it was empty. Immediately she felt horrifyingly sober. The only thing to do now was to try and sleep if she could.

'Dear God,' she prayed, which she sometimes did when she was desperate enough, 'just let me sleep through this night and I'll not touch another drop. Or at least,' she amended, not wanting to commit herself entirely, 'I'll cut it down a bit.'

After that she lit a cigarette, inhaled deeply, then as if in answer to her prayer her eyelids began to droop. So she settled back against the wall and fell asleep, the cigarette dangling from her lips, which eventually fell down on to her coat when she began to snore, sparking off some particles of fluff adhering to it.

The following morning her remains were found amongst what was left of the burnt-out warehouse, quite unidentifiable except for a ring encircling her finger, enscribed 'To Mavis, love Eddie, Dec 1963'.

The Chair

Poet's and Painter's

GEORGE BRUCE

chair – a seat for one person
Oxford English Dictionary
cheer, chear, cheir-chair
Concise Scots Dictionary
καθεδρα – *a seat*
Greek English Lexicon

Greek gives the chair dignity, suggests cathedral,
a bishop's seat, hieratic, 'dim religious light', but
'Poet's Chair?' No! Na! in Scots 'Makar's Cheer'.
frae whilk the makar Robert Henryson began the anely
great, tragic makar's tale in Lallan tongue,
The Testament of Cresseid, screivin in winter,
'I mend the fire and beikit me about
Then tuik ane drink my spreitis to comfort
And armit me weill fra the cauld thair out.'

Poet   Sic a cheer for guid Maister Henryson, teacher,
maun sober be as fits the man, durable, siccar
as the aik frae whilk it cam, its seat comfortable
whaur a man meth set his doup lang hours,
legs nae funcy, at joints tenon to mortise firm,
airms fluent in style, supportive, convenient
for the poet while deep in thocht, or drappin aff,
or in a dwaum seekin solace frae warldly cares,
afore the neist blast o words, thunderin his lugs,
comes roarin tae his pen. Sic a cheer had I
and thocht the seasoned wuid would last for aye.
Syne again a natur it eam to be anither thing.

Wife   It couldna be but him that knocked the cheer
tae kingdom come. Nae meenit still
but raxed himsel, one way an tither,
forard an back, his pen in's nieve,

warslin wi yon cheer, tormentin't, daein
a fandango on the flair, stumpin aroon
the room huntin ae word, a ithers bein wrang,
syne pechin at the desk, heid bowed doon,
he think he's catcht it in his haund,
he's balanced on twa legs, the hinder twa in air,
the puir thing strivin tae haud thegither,
taiglet we his sinews, wrigglin tae get awa.
Sudden he pu's the cheer aneath his bum,
he thinks he's got the measure, the richt beat
o the words: now they'll sing for him, groan,
moan, smile, laugh for him: he's happy,
awa wi't – ower the mune, gone tae
a dear green place (he says) whaur peace
breathes ower a, leavin ahint in sair travail
the cheer that's taen frae him his fevered fears.

Poet   Na, na. I sat me doon on't fine and cosy
cocked an ee at my braw time-piece –
snoozing time for me in my auld cheer
that cam tae me from my good business father,
a man o sense, who had nae time
for flim-flam poesie but 'held straight on
for deals'. He was 'well thought of', respected,
wearin a black top-hat at funerals. Syne
in mid-thocht I'm gruppit frae ahint,
roon my middle and ablow – a randy customer
wha, octupus-like, flings its airms
there's mair than twa, aboot my breist,
twines its legs roond mine – I'm in
a strait-jacket – bangs my heid
shoves it tae this white paper on the desk,
and in my lugs words o the cheer commence:
'Sgriobh! Scrieve! Write!' – the command
in a' three leeds, the ancient tongue, Gaelic,
language of the Garden of Eden (*the Gaels say*),
the Lallan tongue, my ain, aince the King's Scots,
English as spoken here in Scotland: but scrieve what?
Whispers, whispers, 'la chaise du peinture',
The Yellow Chair, Vincent's chair.

In Arles that spring the lark rose
from the cornfield to sing for him.
Skies rejoiced, sang their blue for him.
The petals of the orchard showered about him,
each blossoming on the knife, the brush,
in the chemistry of paint. In Arles
from dawn to dusk the sun shone for him.
He painted the yellow sun. He painted
the sower as the sun drove earthwards
and the hand of the sower was the hand
of the god of creation. He painted
the sway in the corn as the organic
earth-force ordered him. The vault
made its statement, no words for such utterance.
The charge set, the fuse lit, earth leapt,
the onrush in a gyre spiralled the cypresses.
Skies hurried their thunders in oes and whorls,
hurtled him. In his wonderment he became
them. No respite. The eyes of the stars were his,
entered him, force unleashed, leashed,
channelled to brain, hand, encounter
with canvas – all to be rejoiced in. No:
such unfair advantage – a universe expounding
its force, had done so in quake, volcano,
earth-crust opening, basalt flow, rock,
through geological time, now a concentrate
in him, demanding him to contain such violences,
trap all in the small rectangle. There was
blood at his listening ear, blood at his eyes.
His astounded look was in the black cloud of crows
darkening its yellow: but about and about the town
bright undulating meadows, a yellow sea – buttercups,
'I shall paint my little house yellow. I want it
to be the house of light for everyone.
Let the sun walk into my house.'
The sunflowers spoke to him:
'L'oeil du soleil, c'est l'oeil de Dieu.'
I shall put them on the walls of my room.
He put twenty burning suns in the atelier
for glory: their hosannas possessed him,
but in the bedroom 'square deal furniture,

the wooden beds are like fresh butter'.
Two chairs had their beginning in a tree
nearby and in the grasses of the field,
products of the slow labour of country people.
He stared at the chair where Gauguin had sat,
looked long at it where Gauguin had left
his pipe and ash on it. He'd painted the chair;
now he painted a picture of it:
'a wooden straw-covered chair yellow
all over standing on red tiles against a wall'.
Planted now by the painter's hand,
firm, sturdy, settled, no grace
but authority, seen with the eye
of imagination and love it proposes
no time past, no future, but is.

A Domestic Observation

FRANK KUPPNER

An established forty-one-year-old author gets to meet many interesting
   people.
On Saturday, I was in the ten-room house of a fairly successful journalist.
On Sunday, I was in the nine-room house of a likeable teacher of
   literature.
But today, I merely sit in my own room, quietly writing.

The Privacy Switch
MOIRA BURGESS

Nine o'clock, half-past nine, and still nobody has turned up. 'Well, they won't come now,' Sara says. She hopes she sounds sad enough.

But Rory prowls through the flat with his clipboard hugged to his heart. Every time he crosses the hall he checks the privacy switch by the front door, in case it's glowing red. 'If it was on,' he frets, 'they could be buzzing and we wouldn't hear.'

'They're not buzzing. They aren't there.'

'What's happened to them?' moans Rory. 'Batley said they'd come! Mr Macdonald! Mr and Mrs Ferraro! Mizz Carberry-Jones!'

'It's a buyers' market after all.' Sara stands by the high front window with the night city unrolled at her feet, glittering for miles and miles, white and gold and green. 'I wish we weren't selling,' she says.

'Sara!'

'Sorry.' Though she isn't. 'I'm just being —' Awkward? Bloody-minded? Myself? 'Moody.' He can't quarrel with that.

He does worse, loping across the big room to hook his free arm round her shoulders. 'Perhaps you're —'

'No, I'm not!'

He's cast down. His plans are getting out of synch: buy house, start baby, sell flat, live happily ever after with two-point-four bright children running in and out of the patio doors.

She could tell him in three words that everything's on course after all. She doesn't.

'Maybe it isn't going to sell,' she says.

'Early days yet.' There's an edge to his voice.

'Yes.' Too soon to be worried, or excited either. In a few days she'll buy the kit. She doesn't need it. She's sure. But the next bit: to Rory and Sara; she isn't sure of that.

Though they've been waiting all evening, they jump when the buzzer rasps in the hall.

'Hello?' gasps Rory into the speaker. They can hear only uncertain murmurs four floors below, at the security door.

'Hello!' Rory snaps.

A girl's voice, distorted by the sound-box, quacks, 'We've come to see the flat.'

'Did Batley send you?'

Only a confused noise, mixed with the grind and hum of buses and cars.

'They'll go away again,' observes Sara. She leans forward and says, 'Hope you don't mind us asking?'

'Naw, that's okay,' a boy's voice says.

Sara laughs, though Rory isn't pleased. Yes, well, that's the answer she invited. 'Come on up, top flat right,' she says, and presses the button. As often happens, there are sounds of fumbling and mutters of distress. 'Push the door while the buzzer's sounding,' she instructs them, and this time hears them begin to climb the stairs.

'They won't do,' Rory says.

'You can't possibly be sure of that.' She pauses. 'And it's not as if we've had anybody else to view.' She knows it will annoy him and yet she says it, which isn't how things should be. Not even how they used to be. She knows that too as she opens the door.

True enough, in Rory's terms, they won't do. The young man is wearing what once was quite a good suit. Sara's mind flicks back to jury duty in the High Court: a young fellow in the witness-box, good suit, collar and tie. Lying himself blue in the face, as it transpired.

The young woman is faintly shabby and crumpled. Like a student, but there's something more. Rory's nostrils quiver like a cat's. Yes, there's a very faint smell. Smoke and skin.

Sara holds the door wide. 'Come in,' she says. 'You're the first tonight.'

Rory gulps behind her, but what can he do? 'Recession, we can't be choosy,' Batley has said, if not in so many words. He steps back into the hall and the down-at-heel girl steps in. 'This is lovely,' she sighs, a bird nestling home.

The boy stays on the landing, inspecting the sturdy folded-back leaves of the storm-door. 'That's a good thick door,' he says.

'Very secure! Not that we've had any break-ins! Not in this street!' Rory isn't quite his usual fluent self. He has a list of selling-points on his clipboard, but the storm-door isn't one of them.

'We've still got the original key,' Sara says. 'It's nearly a hundred years old.' Like the delicate plaster cornices and the curlicued fireplace around their inefficient old gas-fire. 'There isn't a fireplace *at all*!' she'd discovered, viewing their new house with its plain walls, plain ceiling, plain accurate right-angles between. Rory, crooning in a cupboard over the central-heating boiler, hadn't heard, or anyway hadn't replied.

But if the storm-door might be a selling-point he won't let it go. 'Nobody could get through that door,' he assures the young couple, trembling in his sincerity, because he has a hell of a big bridging loan and they're the only people who've come to view.

'I like that,' the boy says, thumping a panel to test its strength.

Make the most of what they like, Batley has said. Rory leaps in: locks, bolts, entryphone, a desirable top-floor Alcatraz. Sara wanders into the sitting-room, over to the front window where the wide city sprawls on its hills. She hears Rory flicking the privacy switch up and down. 'When the red light's on, the buzzer doesn't sound,' he's explaining. 'We use it at night. Or any time, really, when we want some peace.'

She remembers times they've used it. Mid-morning, Rory unexpectedly home. Before dinner, courgettes cooking to mush. In the kitchen; on the sitting-room rug. She folds her hands at her waist. Lock up, put on privacy switch, go to bed, try for a baby. But when was the last unscheduled time? She can't remember that.

'Elections!' Rory is laughing. 'Christian Aid week!'

She remembers the last time now. It wasn't for love. Rory rushing in, indignant, slamming the privacy switch to red.

'There's a bag-lady downstairs. Begging! In this street! Where are you *going*, Sara?'

'We're out of semi-skimmed.'

'Wait till she's gone. I won't have her pestering you.'

'I can cope, darling.' But, running downstairs, she'd been a bit edgy, looking out for the pesky bag-lady through Rory's eyes.

She'd glimpsed him at the high window above her, watching anxiously to see that she made it to the corner shop and back to their safe love-nest. This is really bloody silly, she thought. She had a pound coin and a fiver in her purse.

She remembers the bundled sheaf of grey-black coats and hair. She remembers the crisp feel of the note folded in four.

She knows what she did, but not why. She knows that people change; some people; not Rory. She doesn't know what, if anything, she's going to do now.

They're all in the sitting-room at last. 'Right!' says Rory, wielding his clipboard. Their money's as good as anybody's, he has evidently decided. 'I'll just mark your names off the list. You must be Mr and Mrs Ferraro.'

'Must we?' the young man says.

Rory blinks. 'Mr Macdonald and –?' There's no ring on the girl's hand.

'What is this?' says the young man. 'We want a house. That a crime or what?'

There's a long, long silence in the shadow of the For Sale sticker which Rory hadn't wanted Batley to put on the window. 'Is this a serious enquiry, Mr –?' Rory says in a faint voice.

'The name's Mick,' says the boy. 'Mick an Jen. An aye, it's serious.' And he repeats, 'We want a house.'

'We need a house,' says Jen, solid and sweet-faced at his elbow. Sara sees that the buttons on her worn old coat are pulled tight over the beginnings of a bulge.

Rory opens his mouth. What's he going to say? Sara steps forward in front of the clipboard, 'Then you'll want to see round,' she says.

Rory has practised the grand tour assiduously and made her practise too. Though he sulks behind them, it goes like crazy clockwork: new windows, original cornices, open outlook, carpets included. 'Plenty power-points,' Mick approves.

'A shower, I like a shower,' comments Jen in the bathroom. She also admires the deep hall-cupboard.

'For your hoover,' Mick suggests.

'*My* hoover! Oh thanks a bunch!' cries Jen. They laugh and cuddle in the hall while Rory glooms.

In the bedroom it's even better, though worse from Rory's point of view; no way does he want to sell to them, but what if nobody else comes? They strut before the full-length mirrors. 'Two fitted wardrobes,' points out Sara, 'his and hers.' Mick opens a wardrobe, though Jen makes him slam it shut at once.

'Aye,' he says, 'we'll need all of that.' Sara sees Jen's mouth tighten briefly. He goes on to say, 'What about weans' clothes, though? Later on like?'

'No worries,' says Jen, hugging his arm. 'This is only a starter flat, okay? We'll move on.'

She stumbles a bit over 'starter flat', but 'That's right,' he agrees. They smile at one another. They're an attractive young couple, shabby as they are. As they turn to leave the bedroom Jen lays her small dirty hand, just for a moment, on the pillows of the king-size bed.

'When could we move in?' demands Mick, in the hall again.

Rory chokes on his pencil. 'Oh, soon,' Sara says. 'We've bought a house already.'

'Why are you moving?' whispers Jen. 'This is so nice I'd never want to move.' And that, unlike 'starter flat', comes out natural and clear.

Loftily, Rory explains, 'We want a house with a garden. We're hoping to start a family.' Possibly he hasn't noticed Jen's tight coat. 'No fun for Sara with a baby,' he proceeds, foot firmly in mouth, 'stuck in a top-floor flat all day.'

Jen doesn't object to this, but Mick's thick brows draw down. Suddenly there's a tension in the hall. Jen takes his arm again. 'It's all lovely,' she says. She's been practising too. 'We'll let you know.'

'We haveny saw the kitchen yet,' says Mick.

Jen assures him that it will also be lovely. He's not for turning. 'The kitchen,' he says, 'afore we go.'

Rory clears his throat. 'The kitchen. Yes,' he says. 'Now I should explain it isn't a fitted kitchen. Not yet. We eat out a lot, you see.'

It isn't clear whether Mick does see. He glares at the kitchen, perfectly adequate but not quite at the pitch of perfection which the bedroom has attained.

'For instance, there's no dishwasher,' admits Rory. But this too he has polished up into a selling-point. 'We're offering the flat at a very realistic price,' he stresses, 'just because of that. We feel that you –' No, he can't quite say it. 'We feel that the purchasers will want to plan the kitchen from scratch. To their own requirements. Exactly.' There, he's got that over beautifully. He smirks at Sara, who doesn't respond. She's watching Mick.

'Right,' Mick says slowly. His eyes gleam. 'So we can dae what we like.'

'Of course! Of course!' cries Rory. No doubt he remembers marching round with Sara on viewing expeditions, talking up a storm about fitted worktops and bathroom suites. Everybody does it. It's part of the viewing routine.

'Okay!' says Mick. 'We'll take that oot for a start!' He kicks the gas-cooker rather hard. Rory jumps.

'That's lovely. We'll phone,' gabbles Jen, trying to tug him towards the door.

He doesn't move an inch. 'What's that we seen up the town? Halogen hobs? That's what we'll get. An a dishwasher, that'll go in there. Nae tumble-dryer? My God! We canny dae without that!'

His voice gets higher and higher. He's moving now all right, round the kitchen, thumping here and there. He makes an actual dent in the washing-machine lid. 'Naw, a washer-dryer. A great big freezer, that yin's far too wee.' He plants a kick on it. He vaults up on to the kitchen table and from there he stabs a pointing arm towards the four corners of the flat. 'We'll have Sky! A video in every room! We'll have a bidet!' he screams. From his breast-pocket he pulls a filthy old cheque-book that he's maybe found in a skip. 'We'll take it! How much?' he howls.

'Stop it! Stop it! Stop it!' cries Jen, and bursts into tears.

Mick jumps off the table and Rory flinches, but Mick dashes past him into the hall. There are vomiting sounds. Sara hopes he's made it to the bathroom. She gives Jen a glass of water and holds her while she sobs.

'Sorry, I'm awful sorry,' Jen is trying to say. 'I telt him we shouldny – It's the third this week.' She sniffles. 'We seen one in Fairisle Street an another in High Patrick Road.' Sara knows the names but she's never been there, not even driving through. 'We couldny afford them. Then he says, Come on, we'll try this yin!' She pauses. 'We canny afford *anything*,' she says. 'It's all a kinna game he plays.'

Rory is very, very angry. He's keeping it down, Sara knows, for fear of Mick. 'Wasting everyone's time!' is all he says. There's a strand of spinach, Sara detachedly notes, caught between his front teeth.

'Sorry,' Jen says again. Mick comes trailing back from the bathroom. Jen looks at him, a long look. 'Actually,' she says, 'I'm no sorry. You can see we need a house.'

'I know,' says Sara, She's going to say 'I understand', but how can she? She says, 'I'm pregnant too.'

She sees Rory's stunned face, but nothing like so clearly as she's seeing Jen and Mick.

There's no trouble as they leave. Mick's drained in body and soul. Sara makes a move to follow them, but Rory pulls her back.

'Sara, is it true?'

She nods, and he nods in return. He's smiling. For the next forty weeks or so, she realises, he'll say he understands her wildest moods.

After that?

They hear a wordless shout two floors below, echoing round the stairwell; Mick's returning to himself. Rory explodes into action, hauling the storm-door shut, turning the massive key. 'All they want is a house!' she cries. He locks and bolts and bars and slams on the chain.

'It shouldn't be allowed,' he's saying, running about the hall. He grabs up the phone and stabs at buttons, but stops before the number's through.

'Batley won't be there. And it's not his fault,' he says, 'exactly.' The receiver shivers in his hand. He turns to her and bleats, 'Treble nine or what?' She sees the spinach still stuck in his teeth.

She shakes her head and he slowly puts the phone down. For a long minute she hopes he's got it. They stand in the hall, Sara and Rory, once together and now on different roads. Jen and Mick are there as well;

they'll never leave Sara now.

If they're with Rory too, she thinks, there's maybe still a chance.

But he says, 'Let's go to bed. It won't hurt, will it?'

'Bed?'

He strokes her hair and his eyes grow narrowly merry. 'What about the sitting-room rug?' he says. 'Remember?'

He's beaten off the villains and everything's safe again, his house, his wife, his baby, his world. He turns towards the sitting-room, where they'll lie above the panorama of the city. A million lighted windows. A million closed doors.

'In the morning,' she says desperately, 'perhaps we can find out how to help them.'

'Right. Sure.'

From across the hall she has a clear view of his hand going out to the privacy switch and flicking the light to red, so that if somebody comes to the door he won't hear.

am pasgadh na bliadhna 1992
AONGHAS MACNEACAIL

am pasgadh na bliadhna
air cabhsair dhùn éideann
na beòil, na beòil
gun cheathach feirg air an anail
na déircich –
sgillinn airson biadh ars iadsan
gun cheathach feirg air an anail

tha bristeadh ann a seo
tha bristeadh ann a seo

in the folding of the year/hogmanation 1992
AONGHAS MACNEACAIL

in the folding of the year
on edinburgh's pavements
the mouths, the mouths
no vapour of rage on their breaths
the beggars –
some coppers for bread they say
no vapour of rage on their breaths

there's breakdown here
there's breakdown here

Burden

TESSA RANSFORD

Elephants of polished teak, ivory tusks,
carved by Indian *mistri* cross-legged in the dust,
wrapped in his *chadar* and carried to the station,
spread out on the platform to catch the dulled eyes
of British families travelling in May
to the hills, or returning in September
after the Monsoon . . . a few annas thrown.

The craftsmanship is perfect and detailed:
one elephant pulls and the other pushes
a log of teak as big as themselves.
Mighty civil servants, the leader takes the strain
and the other puts his weight behind the task.
The white man's burden? Elephantine
to build and bridge, to heal and teach,
to manage and manufacture,
to transport and distribute.

Ships brought them to a bitter post-war Britain.
They settled as they could in villages and suburbs,
market towns and terraces, but on their mantelpieces
teak elephants were still and still at work.

Passed on to the children who had played with them
from house to house, the tusks now loose,
the burden was inherited along with carpets,
silver, jewellery.
               All I have is from the India
of my parents. Surrounded by it I live
far from it. Chained to the log I cannot move.

Bus to the Edge of the Real World
HUGH MACPHERSON

The bus goes on and on, to some remote suburb of London. I've lost track now. It hardly matters. And Martin still goes on too. About how he's never a man to be told what to do by any woman like me. He is, of course. But that's precisely why we're going through this. This scene. With the passengers conscientiously staring out the windows. Not involved. Or perhaps just too kind to add to the pressure.

I try not to look at them either. Just at my shoes, and out of the window at the houses, some with gardens that seem cool and shady and cheer me up for a moment as we go by. Lilac. Or is it buddleia? Waiting for that voice to start up again. So, it's the age-old question. How did we get here?

Running away, in my case. Running away from a home where people constantly tried to control one another, where exchange of insults was followed only by silence. And then finding out running away caused silence too.

I just wanted them to talk about it first – the parents of friends, my teachers, the people at the youth centre. Wanted them to agree to notice that there was something wrong, that I looked like someone sleeping on friends' floors, too tired to take in much of what was happening. So that their talking to me would be an offer of help, a step towards me. Something I could take with dignified relief. Because I wanted to talk about it so much. I was afraid of having run away, immediately I had done it. I was afraid of going back, too. I was scared of all the things that could happen from which I had no protection now.

But they wanted me to come to them. To make a sort of application. Something they could consider from their side of the desk, as adults, as professionals. Not like talking to them just as any other people, but as people with status, people who were established in the place where they stood, and could afford the risk of talking to someone floating loose in the world, like me. Instead of speaking to a friend, it was to be like talking to a doctor, to the bank, to the post office – any of those places where you just exchange tokens of conversation which have no meaning except for one impersonal piece of business.

And this way of course they could say: 'Well, she never spoke to *us* about it. If she'd wanted help, I'm sure she would have said. She obviously had her own plans from the start.' They didn't even have to be defensive: much better, they could be disapproving. I'd had my chance. I could have gone to them and received their attention, if I'd hung around their conversations like a collie dog jumping for attention, trying to interrupt. So, if I hadn't bothered, it was because my troubles weren't real.

Is it more difficult for girls to run away? Everybody talks as though it were, gives grim looks of salacious worry about the 'obvious dangers'. But it's just the same for everyone. Frightening. Lonely. Dirty. All the time for interesting things taken up by having to find somewhere to wash, somewhere to sleep, somewhere to leave your things where they won't get pinched. Thinking about food. Knowing that offers of help are usually just abuse from people who normally have no power, but now find someone strayed out from the herd and see a chance to finally impose themselves. Perhaps we'll be too weak or naïve to resist in time.

The girls at work now ask about it at rest times, their eyes ready to watch me in enjoyable horror while I produce 'revelations'.

'Is that right, Gillian, that you had nowhere to live for a while, that you were living . . . well, you know, on the Embankment benches?'

They want to say 'on the streets', but they don't dare in case I take offence and won't talk.

'No, Gill, but seriously. What was it like? Was it really awful? There was a brother of a friend of mine did that, and he had real trouble, I can tell you.'

I begin to tell them about the restaurant where I ended up working for a time. But they're disappointed about that, try to get me back on to the times before I found that job.

'Yeah, but that was all right then, Gill. At least you had a place, and other people to talk to. It must have been much worse before.'

But it wasn't, in some ways. At least you did what you wanted within the limits of what there was. In the restaurant, one met the same sort of self-assured pushy people I'd run away from. And this time the relationship was even more clearly established. They were on top and we waitresses would do what they said. If we didn't then quite simply we weren't good workers. In which case we would be sacked. Perfectly simple and straightforward in their eyes. Either we backed up their view

of themselves, in every way that we spoke, in every part of our sub-
missive behaviour. Or we had no job, no money, no food and no place to
stay. Can't say fairer than that, can you? It was the way the world
worked and we'd have to learn it.

Because, of course, they didn't just go to that place to eat. They went
there to polish up their image of themselves, see themselves reflected as
important people in the behaviour of others.

They marched in there straight off the morning train, carrying their
newspapers so you could see what view of the world they'd settled on
years ago.

They strode to their usual tables, with the serious commanding gazes
of those accustomed to be in charge. A judicious look at the menu. A
rapid decision on what was required that day. For with them, it couldn't
possibly be a question, you see, that they simply fancied having porridge
or cornflakes that morning. It was: 'We've got a full schedule of meetings
today, my dear, so I think it had better be the full English breakfast to
match.' All in this impersonal style, part of a process where they just
naturally happened to find themselves assigned the leading role. And
they'd give a quick 'so there we are, my dear', smile to allow you in, for
one little moment, to the excitement of being a key man.

Then, while they waited, there was the careful scanning of the
newspaper, the world-weary sigh at certain articles, the 'I can hardly
believe it' shaking of the head at others. But if the opening plate of
porridge took too long, then there would be a tortoise-like raising of the
head out of the shell of the paper to hiss with increasing anger: 'Excuse
me, I did order a good ten minutes ago now. I wonder if you can get this
sorted out quickly. I have to be away at a quarter to precisely.'

The fountain pens would come out and they would carefully jot down
notes on tiny pieces of paper sandwiched in leather holders edged with
gold-coloured metal. A quick underlining and a nod of approval at what
they had written, and they would carefully fold the notes into their
wallets.

Finally we would get them all sorted out, and have them slurping
away contentedly under the gold-rimmed half spectacles and the
moustaches. And if we saw merely a middle-aged man crouched over a
bowl of cornflakes he was evidently in a hurry to get down, that was just
our inability to see how the real world functioned. For he knew perfectly
well that he was a senior executive, a captain of industry deciding the
world's course and the fates of many juniors, powering his way through
a pre-committee breakfast. Taking in the relevant world news from a
leading ('perhaps *the* leading') world newspaper, before he set out, for

the benefit of others, the company's operations in the world.

That was the most surprising thing. Not that these people were constantly playing big boys' games, as Carol, my friend of the time, would put it, spitting out the words as she shouldered her way into the kitchen with yet another tray loaded with dirty plates. After all, that was what I had run away from in the first place. But what was disturbing was that most of the adult world seemed to be playing along too, to have agreed to take it all seriously. If ever we hinted to the manageress that we found these late onset lunch monitors and school prefects stuck up or humourless, she was shocked. It showed we were not only menial but foolishly, incurably so. All that stuff about people being equal was just what one said. It meant nothing. We were not the equals of these people, and we would never have the chance to be superior ourselves if we couldn't even work out how things stood in the world.

Women sometimes came, of course. The men who knew them would rush forward to be gallant, shouldering out of the way any waitress who happened to block their path. There were ambitious ones who dressed in pin-stripe jackets and skirts to show that they formally subscribed to the world of men's games. And there were the wives with expensive dresses who just happened to be coming up to town this morning, and were joining in before going off to Harrods. If business came up, their husband's colleague would ask them in gallant politeness: 'And what do you think of all this then, Mrs B?' And they would say hopelessly, 'Oh, I agree with Ken on this one.'

But neither type paid any attention to us as we rushed around with our bowls of this and that and the plates of greasy fries. They usually ate nothing themselves.

Martin delivered things, three times a week, to the restaurant. That's how I met him. I was nearly going to say I liked him for his smile, when I heard the phrase again in my head. And realised that it sounds exactly what the power-breakfast executives would expect 'the little woman' to say about her man. What I meant was that he wasn't like them. He wasn't forever calculating how to get something. For them, a smile was a special twisting of the face delivered on certain occasions, to show one was being gracious, or prove one had a sense of humour, or reward an employee without cost for a useful action. To do it, one first thought carefully, in order to make sure the situation demanded this response. Then, having checked, one gave the nerves the necessary instructions to make the muscles move.

Martin smiled because he enjoyed things, because he felt good, because he wanted you to feel good too.

Carol said to me one morning, in one of those brief pauses between one rush and the next: 'Your Martin was here earlier.' I waited. She knew we were going out that night. 'All done up in his new suit. I said to him, "You look like you're waiting for a girl to come along". And he went all serious and said, "I've got one". All indignant. I was going to say that was what I meant, but I realised he'd taken it the wrong way!'

Carol and I looked at each other and smiled, and it was a moment of understanding as well as friendship. We both liked him, and she'd been pleased to see he looked good in his new outfit. But it wasn't blind affection on either of our parts. For me it was a love that could see what it was going to have to put up with. At that moment we both saw him very clearly. Liked him with his faults, or so we thought, liked him for being uncertain of himself.

The next time he came, there was a motorbike on fire in the next courtyard. They couldn't work out if the electrics had gone wrong or if someone had deliberately set fire to it. But the tank had just gone on fire and a little blue flame was beginning to shoot up. Martin, all macho cool, got a blanket from somewhere and walked calmly across and smothered the flames. Then he wheeled it away to a safe spot. There was some applause from the office workers and messengers standing around. He went pink with embarrassment and pleasure and came over to where Carol and I were. He couldn't work out why I was so angry with him.

'I did the right thing, didn't I? I did what needed to be done. I thought you'd be pleased.'

But I wasn't. 'Don't you see,' I said, 'I want you, I don't want a hero, and particularly not a dead one or one so covered in burns he'd never be himself again. If they had ordered everyone to stay away just now, the insurance would have paid up on the windows and the bike and the cars around. Much better than having them full of gratitude and only sorry that they couldn't thank you personally because you were no longer with us. Leaving me to look at your photographs on the wall.'

'But it didn't happen like that. It was all right, and I did what was needed.'

'It wasn't all right by me,' I said. 'It's pure luck you're still here.' But he wouldn't see. And it's true, if they wanted to send him away to 'do what was needed', if the people in command from behind their news-papers felt their position required defending by young men with guns, he'd go and not even resent it.

Carol watched us carefully, saying nothing, but being there, offering what support she could to both of us. I believe she thought I was being rather difficult. But the truth is that Martin, though he's free of any attempt at the 'real world' of domination, has no suspicion of it.

And it's hard, of course, to be free from it entirely. Perhaps some days, walking home from the restaurant across the hot London parks, when all the business world was sweating in its offices, you could find moments when everything was given over to enjoyment of the afternoon, without the need to be part of some further plan. A time when small children were the centre of attention in prams and go-carts, the canopies over their heads like the ceremonial coverings held over kings, the wind sweeping across the chestnut trees an event to be appreciated in itself. But a few hours afterwards, the business world would be driving home in its motorised columns to the suburbs, the babies banished to their rooms, the motor-mowers scything the daisies, and the households would revolve once more around the office and the eternal question, 'how was work today then?

And now on the bus, still in the sphere of influence of the 'real world', we continue to head for disaster somewhere on the outskirts of London.

'I've never done anything but follow my own way,' Martin continues, 'ever since I left my mother all those years ago. Always made my own way. And if you don't like that, then you can just follow your own. That's how it is. And how it's going to be.'

He's not drunk. But he might as well be.

I believe the others think I've got one of those hopeless passions, that will put up with anything, even relish it. How can I tell them that I see him clearly but still think something good will win out? That I blame not him but the 'real world'?

I can't. And maybe I'm wrong anyhow.

Into the middle of the hot day, there comes a picture in my mind of a scene from when I was very small. Of a coal-cart and horse, one of the last in our district, turning slowly out of a yard in the snow, the flakes drifting and both horse and man moving calmly forward, wheel-marks in the snow running smoothly behind them, straight like a railway line. And silence, absolute silence, except for a constant whisper of snow in all the bushes and trees and walls. No sound of wheels or hooves. Just snow gathering and the cart moving forward as in a dream.

The conductor rings the bell for a request stop. 'Any more to get off?' he asks, looking hopefully at Martin.

I think of a house on my own, in one of those empty village streets where cars sweep by in the rain and see no reason to stop. From behind the inevitable lace curtains, I'd look out and think about the walk through the rain to the post office or the co-op. Maybe decide just to stay in on my own space, screened from the street, where listening to the rain, or watching the changing face of the sun on the house walls, would be enough to keep me content.

I look forward to being old and eccentric. A better form of running away. More difficult for others to deal with.

'Any more?' says the conductor again.

'*She* can get off if she wants,' says Martin. The conductor shrugs. And so do I.

Voices: Four Meditations and a Lament
TOM POW

(On words scratched on the windows of Croick Church
in Ross-shire)

1. GLENCAL PEOPL WAS IN THE CHURCHYARD HERE
From Maeshowe to Pompey; from Lascaux to Tobruk:
the ancient mark of momentary presence,
the signature of ghosts. With their absence they paid
for this gaunt landscape, those who sought shelter
in the churchyard, too pious to enter the church itself.
Lit by small fires in the damp, tented graveyard,
the peat-cutting hand cut into the glass. He signed
in another tongue to reach another shore:
they had been broken on their own, their name, a song
already fading. I can still catch his breath
as fist and flint loop across the small diamond pane.
This is harder than breaking rocks! But it must be said.

2. MURDER WAS IN THE YEAR 1845
Call a spade a spade. There are many ways to skin
a rabbit and none knew more of them than they did.
First you must kill it. Deal in facts as the graveyard does:
birth, death – murder. This voice is the bitter whisper
in the wind: you can't shake it this end of the glen.
Though the murder written of here didn't happen here,
as the lament that sings in Wounded Knee was composed
many years before it, and the murder of Kurds
driven like deer was in someone's eyes long before it.
Ten years before Thoreau split the godless world –
on one hand there is suffering, on the other
the 'quiet desperation' through which we live our lives –
this, painfully, was scratched into the wind.

3. GLENCALVIE PEOPLE THE WICKED GENERATION

As if they were another species, someone
from *The Times* spoke for them to the wider world,
told of the wretched spectacle they'd made leaving
their land at last, refugees with carts of children,
the poor supporting the helpless poor. Anon wrote:
*If such as happened here transpired in the south
there would be outrage.* (His pen; their flint.) But they
being damned, damned themselves. Though they grew like rowans
in the rock of the land, their spirits cracked
like firs without it. This voice is the saddest fiction
and they took it to the grave. The wretched of the earth –
shaking the journalist's hand, he thought, like children.

4. GLENCALVIE IS A WILDERS

Passing over a swell of lonely hills that sap
the earlier green of the strath, black cloud shadows
like lids in the sky, close on clear runs of sunlight.
The rubble of an ancient broch can give no shelter here,
nor the ruined sheepfolds pinned to the hills.
The faint light still catches the last of their voices
muted by horse chestnut, sycamore and ash,
though the wind soughing through the tall spruce bites
back the last word. Their backs turn from you now, their carts
move off and they fade, leaving not the pristine world
of Walden, but a hard land that once gave shelter
turned into a land of ghosts, a wilders . . .

CODA: LAMENT

It is above all and beyond all doubt a doleful song,
characterised by a melismatic note, a monotonous tone,
appearing to involve a repetitive attempt
at a drone-like narration of some overwhelmingly sad
                                    and disturbing events
which seem to have affected the home.

The singer's inner agitation is clearly shown
in the way his face appears drained and drawn,
with a fixed smile as ironic accompaniment
                    for such a doleful song.

One is left with the lasting impression
of a man who has been battling with tears too long;
but who, even in exhaustion, cannot cease his lament.
His is the haunting voice of peoples whose futures are rent,
whose stolen past cannot come again.
It is above all a doleful song.

*(From the observations of a musicologist
on an untranslated song by an Aché
Indian whose tribe faces systematic
genocide in Paraguay.)*

The Hert o the City
DUNCAN GLEN

'In Glasgow, that damned sprawling evil town'
G. S. Fraser

I'm juist passin through
late at nicht. I risk a walk doun
through the gloomy tiled tunnel o Central Station
to Argyle Street and the Hielantman's Umbrella*
for auld time's sake.

I see them at aince. Three girls and a wee fella
wi a bleedin heid. He's shakin wi laughter
and the bluid's splatterin on the shop windae.

I'm juist about awa back up the stairs when they're
aa round me. 'On your ain?' 'It's awfu cauld!'
'Ye shouldnae be here by yersel!'

I canna help but notice the smell o drink and dirt.
His heid's a terrible sicht.

I look round but I *am* on my ain.
'Whaur are you from?' 'Preston?' 'You'll know Blackpool?'
Soon he'll hae my haill life story out o me.

'You maun be cauld' and
'Ye shouldnae be here by yersel.'

*Hielantman's Umbrella is the railway bridge over Argyle Street

I offer them some money to get in out o the cauld
but they laugh at the idea. They're no hungry
and there's plenty wine left.

They'll get fixed up themorrow.
It's warm enough unner the brig.

They'd walk me back safe to my pletform
but the polis'll be in the station.

'Ye shouldna be here by yersel!'

The Man who Played with Eric Clapton
ANDREW GREIG

He shouldn't have come to the Heriot-Watt Christmas party. He shouldn't compete for an anxious moon-faced student he didn't even want. He knew who he wanted but they'd agreed when Kim had gone south: no commitment. Wait and see.

Now his opposition yawned and made the decisive ploy.

'As it happens, a long time back I used to play with Eric Clapton. Country & Western! I was on piano, Eric played bass. We were terrible! One night when Eric and I were out of our skulls in Soho . . .'

Who can compete with that? thought Jimmy. Then again, who'd want to?

A foregone conclusion, really, the Man Who Played With Eric Clapton being a senior lecturer, and Jimmy just a former engineering student now wasting himself on the rigs. The victor gyrated away with his satellite hanging on his arm.

Jimmy leant his forehead to the cool plate-glass. It's another dreich winter of discontent. Bitter night-shifts on the drill floor, McGovern drying out up on the derrick, all of us bitching but terrified of losing our jobs. The cohesion's gone, young Kim's in an increasingly foreign country.

He collared a bottle and offered it to a junior lecturer in Fluid Dynamics. She accepted, smiled, said her name was Alison.

It was enough that she was someone.

Kim sat on the shingle and looked up at the stars. Simon and Jeanette were kind enough but way over her head and anyway they had each other. They said they were Anarchists which sounded exciting, but seemed to mean no money, spinning out tobacco in ever thinner cigarettes, playing boring old music and discusssing theorists whose names she couldn't pronounce properly.

Whatever I'm meant to do, she thought, is not a theory. It's not about anger or politics. Better still, not about me.

Lately the world seemed so dismal and coarse, she couldn't bear it being dismal when it was trying so hard to be beautiful. *I need to make,* she said to her secret sharer, *fragments of a world that doesn't quite exist, or one day I'll crack again.*

She wrapped the duvet more tightly round herself and shivered.

She looked along the coast, and a rising moon, bloody and pink, caught her by the throat. The little voice she trusted beyond any other finally spoke.

When will I be complete?

The question had been waiting for her since she was twelve. She waited on. The reply seemed to ring back across space.

Probably never.

Ah. She felt herself waver, as though she were nothing more than a ring blown from someone else's cigarette. She waited for the little voice to tell her how she felt about this.

Fair enough.

She stomped thoughtfully back to the permafrost cottage. In her wee room she lit candles, sat cross-legged on the bed while through the wall Eric Clapton's guitar keened for Layla. She looked at the random objects she'd gathered – pebbles, shells, driftwood, chunks of sea-smoothed glass.

She considered their textures, their weight in her palm and their weight in her mind.

She allowed herself to think of the stone butterfly her father had made after his first breakdown. Then the carvings with which he had whittled away the evenings of his Polish exile. Such intricate workmanship. And such irrelevance, she thought angrily, all decoration like the guitar pyrotechnics blethering through from the kitchen.

She glanced at his carving tools in the corner, gathered half a dozen pieces of sea-glass on to the coverlet, picked up her notebook and let her mind go blank.

There was something here, something she could do. Something to hold in the hand and find life bearable.

Dad.

She opened her pad and began. She worked steadily through the night, without preconception and almost without influence.

When she woke she began again, driven by an energy she'd not known since her dad had met a furniture van taking the corner too wide. And at last she picked up his carving tools, slowly turned them in her hands. She had so far to go, so much to learn. It would take her a lifetime.

Jimmy is on the train back to Aberdeen and the North Sea. Kim's surprise gift is in his pocket, cool and inscrutable.

On the phone he and Kim have talked at length, at considerable length, about their passion for each other and their need for independence, for space. Jimmy has lots of space in him, most of it empty. Kim is so dense and compacted that at times she finds it hard to breathe.

It's best when she's enthusiastic and talking about her new work, her ideas, her toys as she calls them. But for much of the time there seems little place for him.

'Wait on,' she'd say finally. 'Everything's changing. Please wait and see what it becomes.'

Punk has become New Wave and unemployment is over two million and the Government still hasn't fallen. From the train Dundee looks like the grit left in the bottom of a dirty bath when someone's pulled the plug. And he's off to extract the oil that keeps the wheels turning.

Everyone needs work, he reckons, but most of us just find employment. Many not even that. He has no special talent like Kim's. So he needs the money, he needs the grease across his palms.

The gaunt man in the seat opposite has struck up a conversation with the restless woman next to him. When they get to Montrose and the man is still attacking the heresy of Darwinism, Jimmy tries to shut out the interminable monologue by recalling in order every room, hillside or shoreline where he and Kim have made love.

'. . . but before I was born again, I played in a band with, uh, Eric Clapton.'

Jimmy opens his eyes from radiant visions.

'Country music?' he asks.

'Goodness, no! Jazz. Eric was always into jazz. He played drums. We all knew he had the makings of genius. Of course, he's a very rich and very lonely man now, he has lost the way.' He glances at Jimmy's guitar case on the luggage rack. 'And what kind of things do you play, friend?'

'Games, mostly. But I'm trying to give it up.'

Smart arse.

When Jeanette is bored she plays Seventies records and kneads dough with scowling concentration. Her dark eyebrows meet at the crease over her nose. Simon is struggling to re-read Max Stirner by the fire; the music makes it difficult. He carefully rolls another cigarette.

Kim is in her bedroom next door with her hands over her ears. Surely Ian Hamilton Finlay didn't have to work under these conditions. She is trying to work out a technique for carving words that will appear to curve into the depths of the glass, as though slipping away. Would she rather incise ferns on a stone, or simply the word *ferns*? Should she go to art college, or study philosophy, or apprentice herself to a craftsman?

She sighs. She will soon be twenty. Art, Life, Jimmy, Fame – she wants everything and she wants it now. She hopes she's a genius and fears she's another irrelevant poseur.

She goes through to the kitchen, can't find any real tea and has to settle for some fousty flower stuff. 'Fousty flower stuff,' she mutters. Jeanette's eyebrows mate. 'What is?'

'That music. *Boring*.'

They argue. What Jeanette calls meaningful, she calls wallpaper. She says she'd left home to get away from the wallpaper. Jeanette loathes Kim's few records: The Clash, the Banshees, Talking Heads. No tune, no rhythm, no talent. Noise.

'Neo-Fascism,' says Simon, looking up from some tricky dialectics.

'Freedom!' says Kim. 'Punk took a flame-thrower to your precious herbaceous border. It's about being young and pissed off.'

'It's being retarded!' Jeanette shouts over *Living On Tulsa Time*. 'There's too much ugliness as it is. Why add to it?'

'You and your bloody Sixties! That music is as out-dated as your kind of anarchy. Two million unemployed and you're still arguing about the right *not* to work! Anyway, why don't we ever have any real tea? I'm tired of this herbal piss water.'

'"Real" is a social construct,' Simon observes.

'Oh bloody hell –!'

Kim slams out of the kitchen, bangs her bedroom door, sits on her bed and begins to cry. She hates being angry, she dislikes swearing, she despises loss of control. She wants Jimmy's arms round her even if he does have all Bob Dylan's albums.

'If that's the new generation,' seethes Jeanette, 'what are we coming to?'

'An end, probably,' Simon giggles.

Jeanette hurls the ball of dough at his head. He ducks. It thuds against the wall and hangs there. Muffled sobs come through from next door. Simon gets up and carefully peels the flattened dough from the wall and solemnly carries it to her spread across his hands.

'Pizza, then?' he says.

The train chunters towards Aberdeen as Jimmy examines Kim's gift, a chunk of blue sea-smoothed glass. On the flat base there are tiny letters but he cannot decipher them. This is so like her.

'Hold it to the light,' she'd said.

He does so now, and turning it over notices a small moon-shaped clearing in the haze. And when he holds that to the window of the train he can see right through to the lettering on the other side. Mirror writing. Squinting, he can now read the italic inscription.

The ultimate triumph of the moon.

Meaning?

'And don't ask what it means,' she said, 'just accept it.'

'Ta verra much, I'll call it *Inscrutable.*'

The train groans north, the gaunt evangelist drones on. Jimmy puts Kim's offering away.

How is he to understand this new generation's heresies? Among others, for the past decade he has been encouraged by women to be gentle, unforceful, above all considerate in sex. To see it as a kind of extreme friendliness. But Kim doesn't want that.

'I don't want gentle,' she'd said scornfully. 'I don't want forty-five chords and extended solos. I don't want technique, just the right three chords. And I certainly don't want to talk about it.'

He shifts in his seat, disturbed. The magazine he's been flicking through tells him men fear intimacy. It doesn't say we can yearn for it, he thinks, nor that some women . . .

He'd looked into her face, saw white specks radiated through her blue iris, saw the darkness of her pupils swell. He'd thought sex a conscious, cultivated pleasure between equals, not this raw clash.

The ultimate triumph of the moon. What's he supposed to do with that information?

He shrugs. There is a gap of generation between them, and sparks crackle across it. But he will never forget the very few times she made love *with* him.

He squeezes the glass. She has marked him forever, he knows that.

Into her bulging rucksack Kim zips the photo of Jim sitting on a winch looking disreputable and gorgeous. Can a would-be Great Artist want also live with one man in a cottage with roses round the door?

In the past months she has been lonely and slightly loopy, survived it, read and talked and thought, and has the beginning of an inkling of what could – with dedication, application and the right circumstances – be her work. There's nothing more for her here. Time to move on.

So why this sick and sorry feeling?

Jimmy has asked Alison to a Lost Poets party.

He likes Alison. For one thing, she is scrutable. She grew up on his side of the '77 faultline. She is relaxed, ironic and informed, knows about a lot more than Fluid Mechanics. She encourages him to read and think, to extend himself beyond the unhappy limits of Scottish Male. Kim can seem very young and insecure beside her.

He enjoys her company, they can even flirt a little. And he is not in love with her, so there is no anxiety.

Still, he is cheesed off to find her monopolised at the bash by a Recognised Scottish Writer who may be witty and charming (if you like that sort of thing) but whose work, Jimmy increasingly feels, is facile and self-advertising. But the RSW has published three books, and Alison has read them.

Jimmy punishes the free wine while the overrated hack outlines at length, at considerable length, his work in progress to an apparently enthralled Alison. So he shifts the conversation of the obese fraud to music, asserting its ultimate triumph over prose.

The obese fraud agrees. Though others have been kind enough to praise his work, he personally finds more satisfaction playing the flute with the Cecilia Chamber Ensemble. They have a concert next weekend. Perhaps Alison would accept a ticket with his compliments?

Alison, that free-loading sycophant, says if she's free, yes.

'And do you play an instrument, James?'

'Guitars, mostly. Rhythm and bass.'

'Oh, *rock*,' sniffs the tone-deaf geriatric Lothario. 'Not what I'd call music. Mere anarchy loosed upon a deafened world.'

Jimmy steps closer to Alison. 'Maybe it's a generation thing,' he says. 'When Punk came along, at first all I heard was noise – the way The Beatles must have sounded to my parents. Alison,' he adds casually, 'has a huge rock music collection, haven't you?'

Kim has said her goodbyes.

She pulls the front door shut and hears Simon stuff his old Afghan coat along the other side as a draft excluder. She will miss them in the rare moments when she permits herself to look back.

She steps into the night.

Jimmy elaborates. 'Rock music,' he continues, 'is a collection of elementary order with elemental chaos. When it becomes over-elaborate, a new movement like Punk has to come along with the flame-thrower. Then it starts all over again. Dialectics, ken . . .'

Jimmy has lost himself and, he suspects, Alison, in this piffle.

Which may be why, when the Recognised Writer snickers and asks if he's played with anyone we might have heard of, Jimmy replies that years back he played briefly in a band with, uh, Eric Clapton.

Alison draws on her cigarette and examines him through the dispersing smoke.

'Now that is a coincidence,' says the sadistic writer swine, 'because there's someone else here tonight who definitely used to play with Clapton. I'll get him over – you must know people in common.'

He hurries off. Alison catches Jimmy's eye. He shrugs. The Liverpool Poet is brought over. Jimmy offers him a cigarette; he accepts, glances at the fingers of Jimmy's left hand.

'So where did you play with Eric?' he asks. 'What was the band called then?'

The Inflated Ego grins. Alison stirs but stays silent.

'We had a residency in a pub off Gloucester Road, can't mind its name.'

'Maybe The Cock and Bull,' the mass-murderer suggests.

'Jazz?' the Poet asks.

'No, straight down-the-line Rhythm and Blues. We called ourselves . . . Fifth Degree.'

The Liverpool Poet examines his ancient winkle-pickers, pulls on his cigarette and waits for a beat. Poetry, it's all in the timing. He shakes his head slightly then looks up, smiling.

'Yeah, Fifth Degree! Eric was always talking about that line-up. You must know Neil Weeks, the bass player.'

'Neil, aye. You know he works for Saatchi's now?'

'Really? A good man gone straight. Were you there on that famous night when . . .'

The defeated, pitiable, and really quite talented rival implodes and fades.

Kim walks carefully down the track to the road end. It's a starry night, fine for adventuring. The moon has disappeared but it still pulls the tides, she knows that. Her sack clinks and clatters, weighed down with carved stones and shells and glass, sketch-pads and her father's tools.

She breathes deeply, willing the nausea to subside. She can leave anywhere she wants to.

She waits at the road end, the future in her thumb.

Jimmy and Alison are crossing The Meadows on the way to her flat.

'I suppose,' she says thoughtfully, 'a lot of people over the years must have played with Eric Clapton.'

'Lots,' he replies. 'Dozens, I should think. Mostly clapped-out.'

They walk on in silence, swaying slightly. Jimmy shifts his sleeping-bag from one arm to the other as a snuffling sound comes from Alison. Then she is laughing, and he begins to laugh with her because once in a rare while life comes out tickety-boo and the night is full of stars, full of 'em.

'Men!' says Alison. 'Always sticking your neck out when you don't have to. And seldom when you should,' she adds and slips her arm through his.

Jimmy lies in his sleeping-bag on her bedroom floor, listening to Alison's breathing slow and settle. He thinks Yes, we are many. Legions. Hundreds, thousands of us all over the world. We recognise each other instinctively when we meet. And we back each other up, because we're members of that orchestra of incomplete beings – the Men Who Played With Eric Clapton.

'Alison?'

'Yes?'

'What am I doing here and you there?'

She switches on the bedside light. Her smile is only slightly patronising. 'I was wondering when you'd ask.'

She will, he knows, make love in the old manner – unhurried, companionable, harmonious. The earth will not shake, the stars will not be torn down.

The Sleepers

VALERIE GILLIES

They worked a tracklife of fifty years,
These split logs lying under the rails,
Fixed on with cast-iron chairs
Spiked to their timber; sapside upward,
        Waybeams packed horizontal.

        Over the tracks run horses,
        Over the grass, the trains.
        Rivers rear in their courses,
        Sleepers rise, trees again.

The line's dismantled, section's down.
Imagining the future, a man stood
Here, thought another use could be found
For them, if he checked the timber's sound
        And close-grained wood.

Free from deadknots and warping shakes.
He tried the adzeing of the waney side,
How far the creosote impregnates,
What sawing and shifting it takes,
        What pitchpine can provide.

He stood the sleepers up on end,
Butted them together and secured
Those with nine-inch nails driven
Through. Doors and windows open
        At the fretsaw's signature.

He made the sleepers stable to a horse.
The big trees, heartside in, are joined.
Invert an opposite, move a force.
Emerging between standard-posts aligned,
       The racer takes her living course.
As lightrays change, passing through a point,
       The engine is antithesis of horse.

       Over the tracks run horses,
       Over the grass, the trains.
       Rivers rear in their courses,
       Sleepers rise, trees again.

The Marzipan One
CARL MACDOUGALL

After scrimping and scraping and making do, arguing with the Social and going to jumble sales; after the child and five years after she married him because he'd asked and because of the shame; after arguing with everyone who said she shouldn't, she stood at the sink and stared out the window, surprised at how she quivered with anticipation.

He had given her the Elvis *Peace in the Valley* LP for two successive birthdays, a box of chocolates for the Christmas in between and nothing else.

Now it's Saturday afternoon; he'll soon be in and wanting his tea. He comes in drunk and falls asleep. Annie Anderson's man's the same, except he batters her. Never on the face, though she sometimes has to walk funny because of the bruises; she'd been taken to hospital four times with bleeding; everybody heard the screams.

All week, she comes in from work, watches the telly, reads in bed and puts out the light when she hears him on the stair. Once they met on the street: 'Hello,' she said, surprised at herself being pleased to see him. Then there was nothing. 'See you later,' she said, and as she was walking away he asked, 'Is this you doing the shopping?'

They always eat in silence. He says 'That's me,' before going out. His habits are established. He wakes around eleven, drinks a can of beer, gets up and sometimes eats a bowl of cornflakes. He's out by twelve and back around three. He sleeps till five, watches television, eats half a meal at six and goes out, coming in around midnight. He never asks for money and she knows he sometimes works. He keeps the Giro.

'This is your bingo night,' he said.

She wondered if he would care, hurrying to wash herself, making sure everything was in place, good clothes beneath her old coat.

She sat beside a girl four or five years younger, pregnant and without a wedding ring. She looked healthy, her hands resting on the lump. It hardly ever bothered her. She sometimes remembered trying to waken

him and walk downstairs; the screaming in the close and the doctor with
the funny eyes who told her, 'It would be for the best. We don't think
you should have another pregnancy. If it went the full term, and that is
unlikely, but if it did you could be very seriously ill. We'd have to take
you into hospital for the last three or four months and frankly we don't
have the beds. It's your decision and we don't want to influence you
one way or another, but we feel you ought to be acquainted with the
facts.'

He never asked what happened to the baby, conceived after a party.
She had to tell him. She was sure he didn't know about the operation
either. She didn't feel right; even after all that time, she still didn't feel
right, still didn't feel like a woman. She got off the bus early and walked
to the hall.

She didn't like going to the dancing on her own, not like before when
there was a crowd, five or six girls all together, going for a laugh and a
dance. The woman at the ticket desk was getting to know her, she could
tell by the way she smiled.

In the cloakroom she took off her wedding ring. She stood in her
usual place by the door where she could feel she was not participating.
You saw who was at the tables. There was never a crowd, nor was it
especially quiet. Couples moved from the floor to the bar to the door.

The other women seldom spoke. She was younger and did not
participate in their silly games of flirting. The group on stage, four men
and a singer, sounded like what you'd expect, no better or worse. The
singer had obviously learned the songs from records. When there were
words or phrases she did not understand she sang an approximation,
secure in the knowledge no one was listening, though she sometimes
tried to make them listen, with songs she felt suited her voice best, like
Feelin Groovy: 'I'm Dappleton Drow; say, I'm ready to sleep.'

The singer was doing *Save The Last Dance For Me* with a bit of *Kiss Me
Honey Kiss Me*. A man with red hands and a smoker's cough stood at the
other side of the door. She stubbed out her cigarette, knowing he was
waiting till the end of the song.

'Right?' he said,

He danced well, not too closely. For a tall, heavy man, he was light on
his feet. Immediately she got the feeling she liked, the feeling of being
enveloped, someone else in control of her movements.

'Staying up?' he asked at the end of the first dance and two dances
later he asked if she fancied a drink.

'I'll need to go. I've to be in by eleven.'

'Married?'

'My mother's not well. I have to look after her. A neighbour's sitting in with her to give me a night out. I was going to come with my pal, but she got a date, so I came on my own.'

'Where do you live?'

'Possil.'

'Can I see you home? Let's have a drink, then we'll get a taxi.'

He started sentences and wouldn't finish them. She said silly things to encourage conversation. He seemed nervous. Men usually were unsure of themselves, looking over, laughing and nudging each other in the dance hall. Wee boys later on. 'Just drop us here,' she told the driver.

He paid and when he turned she thought he was going to say he remembered something he had to do. 'We'll go up a wee bit,' she said before he could say anything. 'Not far to go. Just up here, a couple of closes.'

She could feel his tension and knew his palms were sweating, wondered about opening his shirt to smell all of him. 'This is it here,' she said and walked into the back close.

There was a couple of steps down to the alcove at the back of the stairs. He was beside her. She turned and smiled. He grabbed her hand and together they went into the dark. His face was rough and she ran her hand round the short hair at the back of his neck, pushed herself to him and against the back wall. His hands were wet, overwarm as he pushed his way up her skirt and fumbled with himself at the same time. She opened her legs and undid the buttons on the front of his shirt, rubbing her nose into his chest. This was a sudden thing. He went in quickly, pinning her against the wall. She felt the cold stone and he stopped moving, stood still. She stopped, hoping it wouldn't happen, hoping he wasn't going to come. Again he shoved himself against her, rougher this time, his clammy hands holding her up, her feet off the ground. She held on to the back of his neck, both hands around the stubbly hair, her face in his chest, when she felt it seep round to the top of her legs. It had happened. He kept going though she could feel him getting limp. 'Sorry,' he said. This was different, someone nice.

'It was fine,' she said. 'You must have been ready for it.'

He didn't answer. Funny how men were embarrassed to talk about it, as though their performance was under scrutiny. Once he was buttoned up, he didn't know what to say, red and silly in the light of the close.

'You'd better get going,' she said.

'Right then. I'll be off,.' But he didn't go.

'Goodnight.'

'Would you like to go out again?' he said.

'That'll be nice.'

'Middle of the week?'

'Wednesday's fine.'

'Boots corner, seven o'clock?'

'Okay.'

'Great,' he said.

And though she didn't want to know, she asked, 'Are you married?'

'My wife and I don't –'

'That's all right,' she said. 'I'll see you on Wednesday.'

She waited till the footsteps faded, then, sure he was gone, she changed into her flat shoes, dried herself with tissue and replaced the wedding ring. She felt vulnerable, dressing in the back close, worried about getting caught. It was the third week in a row she'd used this close. She'd need to get another soon, another dance hall too.

Walking the three streets back to her house, where she hoped to God he'd be sleeping, she wondered about Wednesday. It was a rule, once and once only. There hadn't been anyone she'd wanted to see again.

It would be hard to find another close; they had doors and entry phones now. There was one near, where she played dolls and houses with Ann Anderson, but it probably had an entry phone like most of the others.

The teacher used to watch her dance. 'You have a gift,' she said. 'Everyone thinks they can do it and few people can. You should ask your father to send you to classes.'

'Who the hell ever heard of anybody going to dancing classes,' he'd said.

'Always remember,' said Miss MacDonald, her favourite teacher, 'girls, remember it's up to you. It's up to you to make the most of things. No one else can do it for you. We all have a special gift. And it's up to us to make the most of it.'

Ann Anderson called herself Annie. She walked funny because of her man. At least he wasn't as bad as that.

Near the close it started to rain.

Climacteric

ALEXANDER HUTCHISON

This time something threatens to give way entirely:
Ridgepole, roofbeam, whatever you imagine as lasting
This time will fail to remember words that fell so bright
And fast about we found no shelter but the storm itself.

Burning branches in stoves and stalls, juniper burning
And the place thick with the smell of it. Star-bane;
Lesion in the thew of space.

Even the confidence of God at knell of the hardest season
Withers and rots away.

These purposes splinter in a rented room;
Intention, surface, prospect before, behind
Is all some thriftless illusion
Drawn down in a trough of queer air.

I can guess at it – tailing, diminished,
Acknowledge a thread of worn profit,
Even an infection slowly taken –

Nature scourged by sequent effects:
No lamp of bronze, no drum
At the cross-tree –
                    Appetite
And intelligence and little else;
Blood loop on a dry beaten run.

Fifth Avenue

ALAN SPENCE

'Shark cartilage,' said Julie. 'It's the greatest thing.'

They'd met for coffee in the basement of Trump Tower. Julie had suggested it as a meeting place. It was convenient, fitted in with the rest of her day, and he didn't really mind. Even if the coffee cost two-fifty and came in a paper cup. Visually he enjoyed the excesses of the place, the red marble, burnished mirror glass, brass handrails. He'd been watching the shoppers glide up and down on the escalators, zigzagging past each other at 45 degrees, gently numbed by piped Gershwin, an ambience from discreet speakers.

'So tell me about it.'

'We'll make it into powder,' she said. 'Freeze-dried. Sell it in capsules.'

'Easy to swallow.'

'Exactly.' If she'd caught his irony she was ignoring it.

'So what's it good for?'

'You name it.'

'Anything that ails you.'

'Don't tell me!' she said, waving her hands. '*Pennies from Heaven*, right? The guy was Steve Martin, the girl was, don't tell me, Bernadette Peters!'

'Got it in one.' He sang it. 'Love is good for anything that ails you.'

She laughed. 'That's the one!'

'So this stuff is a regular cure-all?'

She nodded. 'Speeds up the healing process. It makes sense when you think about it. I mean, when did you ever hear of a sick shark?'

He thought about it. 'When did I ever hear of a sick aardvark? A sick okapi?'

'Come on! You know what I'm saying!'

He knew what she was saying. 'What are you going to call it? *Jaws?*'

'Neat!' she said. 'Wrong, but neat!'

This time she could definitely sense it, his *attitude*. But she kept talking. 'The really exciting thing about it, I mean for like *now* is it strengthens the immune system. And what with this whole AIDS thing.'

'There's a market out there.'

'Not just that.'

No. Of course not.

He looked up through the slanted glass roof, let his gaze follow the flow of water, lit from below, cascading down the sheer marble wall from four floors up.

'I feel like a character in a Woody Allen movie,' he said.

'Which one?'

'Any one!' He sipped the last of his coffee, dark and bitter through the froth. The dusting of chocolate left a sweet aftertaste. He licked it from his top lip. 'So. Are you coming over tonight, or should I come round to yours?

'Actually,' she said, 'I'm seriously jetlagged. Still catching up with myself.'

'It's always worse coming in this direction.'

'So give me a couple of days, I'll call, okay?'

'Okay.'

Outside in the street she waved down a taxi.

'So,' she said, and she kissed him full on the mouth with a real warmth, and she stepped into the yellow cab, a scene from so many movies, she waved to him as the cab pulled out into the Fifth Avenue traffic, she mouthed *I'll call* behind glass.

Turning he almost fell over a supermarket trolley being pushed along the sidewalk by some skidrow downandout. The man stared at him, eyes hard and bleak. The face was a grey deathshead, the greyness ground in, ingrained in the hollows and crevices, grey skin stretched taut over the skull, the caved-in cheeks covered with rough stubble. In the trolley were the man's belongings. Worldly goods. A cardboard box. A couple of plastic carrier-bags stuffed with old clothes. A blue camping gas stove resting inside a saucepan, beside it a tin of baked beans and, crazily, a sixpack of Coke. Propped on top of it all was a scrap of card, the flap ripped from a carton, and printed on it in black felt-tip, in careful block capitals, was the man's story. HOMELESS NO JOB HIV+ PLEASE HELP.

He felt for the money in his pocket. The notes were all the same size, twenties, tens, fives, singles, so there was no way of telling by touch. He pulled out a bill, relieved it was a dollar, and handed it to the man.

The man took the dollar and looked at it, looked him up and down, looked in the direction the cab had gone, looked up at the gleaming tower, looked again at the dollar, said *Shit!*

(This is from a longer piece called That and a Dollar*)*

Carnival

JOY HENDRY

Look out!
That barrage of balloons
might blind you,
prismatic colours too much for the eye.
They might,
upon an inflated whim
explode in a syncretism of rainbow lightning.

Here there's home among the gaudy throng
for the drunk, the prostitute,
the homeless, the unwanted,
on the grass of a thundery afternoon
to rub shoulders with tidy respectability
and weary workers with trauchled bairns.

That throbbing beat of carnival drums
brainwash the heart,
lull it into sleepy oblivion
before the predatory claw rips home.

Take your hopes to a carnival
at your peril
They will rise sky-high on a tide
of the adrenaline of abandon
beating in so many veins
and disappear into the blue.
There's murder enough in a single breast
How much danger in
a thousand souls intent
in this taking of flesh,
commingling in carnival.

Hæmlis

ROBERT ALAN JAMIESON

Hæmlis, hæmlis,
Mønlicht sleepin on a midnicht loch
hæmlis, hæmlis,
Mønlicht sleepin on a midnicht loch.

Græt gæl distroy wir hæm
mony de'ed, da nicht it micht be de
Græt gæl, græt gæl
Mony de'ed, da nicht it micht be de

Some een say ich hich ich hich ich
Some een sing hullo, hullo, hullo
Some een say ich hich ich hich ich
Some een greet quhy quhy quhy?
Some een say ich hich ich hich ich
Some een sing hullo, hullo, hullo
Some een say ich hich ich hich ich
Some een greet quhy quhy quhy?

an we ir hæmlis, hæmlis,
Mønlicht sleepin on a midnicht loch.
hæmlis, hæmlis,
Mønlicht sleepin on a midnicht loch.

Translated from a poem written by Paul Simon and Joseph Shabalala

Getting There!

JEFF TORRINGTON

As our train dashed through Ep – the shortest station name in the British Rail system – Baskerville, a houndish-looking man, continued to read aloud *The Times:*

'Church clock's three minutes fast; laundry clock's two minutes slow; and the station sundial's bang-on.'

Thanking him, we returned our attention to Cutler, a nail-salesman from Shepney, who, cheerfully waving a couple of sacks of 'Carpenters Friends', hopped blithely on to the platform which was dawdling along at some 90 miles per hour. Incredibly, Cutler managed to keep his feet, or to be more accurate, the stationmaster did, and they are still claimable, complete with galoshes, at the lost property office where many items of no interest whatsoever are to be found. Amongst these are the 6.10 London to Perth train, including the crew and some desiccated passengers who presumably believe they've been diverted via the Channel Tunnel.

'As I was saying,' Struggs in the corner said with typical English reserve, 'After the war I had a squad of illegitimate brats to a fan-dancer from Felixstowe, then, having embezzled my firm, I pushed off to Portsmouth where I got involved in all sorts of unsavoury scams.' His shy glance settled on Puffet. 'Now you look to me like a well-travelled Johnnie.'

Puffet, who was in the act of purloining a painting of Gattersby Marshalling Yard, scowled. 'What makes you think so?'

'Your suitcase, old man,' Struggs said, 'can't see the bally thing for labels.'

'It's not mine!' Puffet said quickly – too quickly – as they say in third-class novels and first-class train compartments. Meanwhile, fields and hedgerows were flicking past outside, which was just as well for things were tight enough in that train without the corridors getting clogged with meadows, paddocks and henhouses. Outside, too, there were cows with depressed heads, and one cow in particular which looked depressed all over. Also outside was this farmer, up to his neck in a silage-pit who still managed a cheerful wave. Pleased by his friendliness, we fluttered our hankies in return.

The old lady sitting to my left suddenly said, 'I haven't read a good hand in ages. D'you mind?'

'Go right ahead,' I invited, 'I'm finished with it anyway.' She peered at my hand then mumbled that my future looked brown. 'Don't you mean black?' I queried.

Her head wagged. 'No, it's definitely brown.'

'Maybe this'll change things,' I said and whipped off my glove.

'Ah, yes. You are about to have a nasty surprise. There!' she exclaimed as the electric bulb above me fell from its holder and scorched a sixty-watt patch on my scalp. Losing interest, she tossed my hand aside. Then, casting a ball of twine on to her fingers, she began to knit a grocery bag.

'Speaking of glass eyes,' said Hoffman, waving a detective novel, 'read this, have you?'

I shook my head.

'Oh, but you must!' he enthused. 'First-class stuff. Most original. This layabout, you see, is the sole legatee in his uncle's will. Mounting gambling debts force the nephew to speed up his relative's demise, for the old fellow remains in disgustingly good health. He attributes this to his yoga practice, but, ironically enough, this is what proves to be his downfall. The nephew imbeds a thorn in his uncle's head-stand mat, a thorn which he has steeped in curare – a deadly French polish.

'Well, the uncle does his yoga routine, concluding as usual with the head-stand: a slight scalp jab, a grunt, and a slithering collapse, not forgetting the traditional strangled groan, and for the uncle it's over. Acting upon Edgar Allan Poe's tip that the best hiding place is the most obvious one, the slayer had concealed himself by standing on top of the TV set. He now hops down from it and, rushing across to his stricken uncle, shoots him with a variety of pistols and revolvers, including a sawn-off shotgun which doesn't work because it's been sawn off at the wrong end. After pinning a suicide note between his victim's shoulders with a steak knife the nephew makes good his escape.

'Inspector Roland, of the Yard, is duly summoned to take charge of the case. But no sooner has he arrived at the crime locus than he is forced to dash off for his annual holiday. On his return Roland taps his way through the massive computer file that has accumulated on the case. By the time he has filtered the available evidence, weighed it in his analytical mind, and puffed thoughtfully on his meerschaum pipe, his annual holidays have come round again. Looking thoroughly fit and tanned, although he has developed chronic bronchitis through his meerschaum musings, Roland decides to visit the murder spot – which by now has become a concreted nursery playground. The suspicion nags at him that he is overlooking a vital clue. As he whizzes down the toddlers' chute, sparks flying from his thought-worn pipe, Roland spots the murderer himself who, it seems, has dutifully returned to the scene of the crime. When his gaze falls upon the inspector the nephew starts guiltily. Roland immediately nabs him for guilty starting in an infants' play area.

'Roland returned to his Crime Caravan from which for many long frustrating weeks there issued like the tip-tapping of a blind man's stick the sound of the computer keyboard as it led the inspector further and further into the dark.

'On an impulse he drops into the mortuary to take another look at the victim. Everything seems to fit into place: the drawer into the cabinet; the body into the drawer; the glass eye into its socket – Roland's pipe leapt convulsively, singeing his moustache. It was the vital clue – not Roland's scorched tash, but the victim's glass eye! There it was, just where wise old EAP said it would be. The inspector has the glass eye rushed to the lab. "Well?" he asks the forensics expert. The technician nods, "There's a dab there all right, sir. A beaut!"

'"As I thought," says Roland. "The killer must've left it as he closed the victim's eyelids."

'"And, if it matches the dabs of that guy you brought in on the guilty-starting rap, the case is open and –"

'"– shut," said Roland as he grimly set off on yet another annual holiday.

'On his return the inspector is informed that the prisoner has escaped. Roland organises a massive woman-hunt, hoping by this ploy to fool the escapee into a sense of complacency. He succeeds; the killer is found stretched across a railway track.

'Pouncing on him, Roland snarled: "I must warn you that your lawyer, after being soundly thrashed, is willing to testify that you made death-threats against the deceased."

'The killer yells, "You can't hold me, copper!"

'"Why ever not?" the dismayed Roland asks.

'The killer waved aloft his gory wrist stumps: "A train knicked my forks off – that's why! Now you can't prove it was my dab on that glass peeper!"

'Despite an intensive search the hands cannot be located. Even forty-eight hours of non-stop torture, which included a Perry Como record being played at the right speed, fail to break their prisoner. Suddenly, one of Roland's assistants has a brainwave. "Saw it in a movie," he says. "Even the bravest can't handle it. All you gotta do is to stick matches under the tightmouth's fingernails, light'm, and afore you know it he'll be singing like a canar –" His voice tails off and next thing he knows he's being bundled down a lethal pothole in Cheshire!

'A chagrined Roland is forced to release his prisoner. Hardly have his boots hit the cobbles than the crook gets someone to dash off a note to the inspector: "You shoulda taken Mr Poe's tip – them glove-fillers of mine were in my pockets all the time!" For Roland this is the end. His career takes a tumble and he winds up French-polishing police truncheons in a flooded basement in Hawick. The novel ends with Roland's mysterious disappearance: "One day," we are told, "Roland sat down in a very obvious place and was never seen again."'

No sooner had Hoffman concluded this saga (a word recklessly imported from Norway during the 'Let Sardines Flow Between Nations Week!') than Puffet leapt to his feet and lugged his suitcase from the rack. But he was too late! His station, making around 95 miles per hour, whipped past – a truly astonishing spectacle since the train had only newly stopped to change crews again. Never have I been on a train so obsessed with crew-changing. In a book by a former loco driver called *With My Tender Behind!*, the blame is laid on a sinister group, the CCA (Crew-Changing Agency) who, the author claims, is directly responsible for non-stopping trains and the dangerous practice of bypassing tunnels. He even goes as far as to say that the CCA have been guilty of planting decoy stations upon the platforms of which the dreaded Crew-Changing Agents, disguised as chocolate-bar dispensers, wait to leap on unsuspecting crews. Reflecting on this, I realised that the station whizzing past our stopped train was probably just another of the CCA's cunning ploys. I mentioned this to Puffet who then made a grab for the communication chain, but no sooner had he tugged on it than with a sighing gush water cascaded on to him from a roof-hole. Immediately afterwards Puffet was led off between two fascist-type porters on a charge of yanking the chain while the train had stopped at a passing station.

I left the compartment and made my way back to the van to see how my luggage was doing. Surprise, surprise – there was no van to be seen, only the guard cowering on a coupling-rod!

'Don't change me!' he implored. 'For pity's sake – don't change me!'

'Where's your van?' I asked him.

'Up front, I guess.'

'Then why don't you go and look?'

'Front ain't my baby,' he declared. 'My job's to protect the rear.'

At that moment an indigant-looking fireman came storming on to the scene. 'Why haven't you gone up to the box to sign the book?' he wanted to know.

'Coz that's your pigeon,' said the guard.

'No it's not!'

'I say it is!'

They began to hurl detonators at each other. Meanwhile, the signal-box which had been edging nearer and nearer to the combatants, finally pounced. It was, of course, a façade for a crack unit of the CCA. The hapless guard and fireman were whisked from sight beneath a sleeper which opened on a hinge after an agent knocked twice and asked for Charlie.

The last stage of the journey was accomplished with only a further 23 crew-changes which suggests that good old BR are indeed 'getting there'. As the rail terminal embraced us in grimy welcome I leapt lissomly on to the platform and found myself immediately enveloped in foam rubber.

It was in this immobile condition that I witnessed a squad of milk churns converging on the unsuspecting crew.

The CCA had struck again!

Another Letter to Lord Byron
ALAN BOLD

So little do we know what we're about in
This world, I doubt if doubt itself be doubting.

Byron, Don Juan (IX:17)

So you were half a Scot by birth, and bred
    A whole one so your heart informed your brain:
A likely story, but you also said
    Truth is stranger than fiction. I maintain
Fiction is stronger than truth; we are made
    By myth and legend. So we entertain
Ourselves by playing games of make-believe:
Our nature copies art. Thus we perceive.

Old Auden (I once met him at a do
    In London, we had both been drinking malt),
Epistolary artist, wrote to you,
    And cocked his snook (or something) to find fault
With you for not being him, one of his crew
    Of righteous poets, the kind who like a cult
Built round themselves. You'd not have been a chum:
The fists of big boys were the war to them.

I've never had much time for poets *per se*;
    The hole-in-corner squabbles, little schools,
And cliques and compacts, bummings-up, hooray-
    Reviews, the puffs, the petty rules
Of current fashions. I have kept away
    From circus-readings with performing fools
Who, led on by their public, think the muse
Is measured by the length of their applause.

For you the poet had to be heroic,
    Involved in life outside the library.
You were a sport, no speculative Stoic;
    You swam and boxed, no armchair wannabee.
I've also boxed, but not to be echoic:
    I learned to fight so none would flatten me.
Brought up with bruisers, I soon learned their game,
And looked on bookish types as rather tame.

As far as sport's concerned I could have held
    My own with you. I'm absolutely sure
I could have thumped you round the ring, half-killed
    You with an uppercut. Dear Lord, what's more
I could have bested you at football, skilled
    From schooldays when I learned to know the score.
At swimming, well – by George, you were no wimp –
You would outlast me even with your limp.

Still, you are dead and I'm alive: we're not
    In competition; I salute your ghost
(You liked the Gothic, Frankensteinish brute)
    And think your spirit's something that we've lost
In times like these, when poets are a lot
    Of poseurs in a lottery of taste.
Manners maketh man, or so they say;
Artistic manners leadeth poets astray.

Enough of poets. I've had enough of those
    Who say they're poets yet calmly kiss the arse
Of social climbers, hoping such a kiss
    Will bring some kind of cash-prize to their verse.
Your lordship's title was not worth a toss;
    It's as a lord of language I endorse
Your name: you used your language to advance
The common cause without which life's pretence.

It's not a cause that's often aired these days:
    The atmosphere's polluted with the breath
Of loud-mouthed dogmatists. They puff their praise
    Of bankers, brokers; they proclaim their faith
In market forces; go down on their knees

To worship profits. Lucre before death
Is their cheap credo. Lo, they dogmatise
About the rule of law, say it's sublime
Then make or break the rules to suit their crime.

In the name of freedom we are told
    We must respect white racists overseas
Who spill the blood of those who mine their gold;
    In the name of freedom, if you please,
We must accept invasions when controlled
    By friendly fiscal powers whose decrees
Make countries items to be bought and sold.
They murder freedom, using freedom's name
As if their profit was its synonym.

In astronomical terms, the Big Bang
    Denotes the universal genesis:
From nothing – crash-bang-wallop – everything
    Exploding outwards from whatever is.
In sexual terms, the Big Bang is the ring
    Of orgasm in the ears. Now Nemesis
Allows the term debased as the small change
Of brokers with their global stock exchange.

You praised 'great Locke and greater Bacon'; we
    Kneel before the name of Adam Smith
(A penny-pincher born in Kirkcaldy).
    Our sacred text's not passed by word of mouth
But written on a bank-note; we are free
    To pocket money if we take the oath
To hand it back, a solemn guarantee.
The cash-flow has become the holy grail:
It works by putting millions on the dole.

These millions: thousands could not give a fart
    What happens to them. They are filed away
As figures, mere statistics on a chart,
    Projections to be screened another day.
Statisticians can remove the heart
    More skilfully than surgeons in their way;
They paper over wounds, they cover scars
In jargon, then they seal themselves in cars.

You see the unemployed in every pub
    (At least I do, I don't suppose you drink
These days). You talk to Mr Thingmybob
    Who tells you, with a dash of doublethink,
How blessed he was when he held down a job;
    Hard work, a wage, watch telly and get drunk.
There's more to life than living week to week:
If he'd grasped that, he wouldn't be so meek.

We're governed by a rigid rule of thumb
    That puts down millions, rubs their faces in
The social shit: they will not overcome
    The foul smell of corruption, they're flushed down
The shithouse, washed away like filthy scum
    While brokers do their business on the throne.
For every bit of business there's a price
The millions pay as human sacrifice.

They ask too little, everywhere 'the wealth
    Of nations' is held by the grasping hands
(That rule of thumb, that fingertip of filth)
    That strangle promise, handicap the minds
Of millions in the global commonwealth,
    Condition them to cow to the commands
Of those who measure their financial wealth.
The few pile up the profits, while the rest
Bow down to them and wallow in their waste.

It sounds so simple to reserve the roles:
    The millions to the millions, you knew that.
It sounded even simpler to your pals
    (Like Shelley). See the debris of defeat:
The broken strikers, the opinion polls,
    The pin-up press, the beggars in the street.
It's not a question of who's left or right:
The brokers make the rules, arrange the fight.

Broker versus striker: the bell goes,
    The striker lashes out, the referee
(A brother broker) won't allow such blows.
    The broker throws a right hook: on one knee

The striker drips blood from a broken nose.
    He struggles to get up, a count of three
Is called, he shuffles forward, gets in close
And shakes the broker with a bellyful:
The broker is the winner on a foul.

That, we are taught, is stark reality:
    The winner takes the prize, the loser takes
His humble place in our society.
    The winner lifts his holy grail and breaks
The heart of his opponents. So, you see,
    Our human nature makes the same mistakes
It did in your day. Progress is a myth:
Existence still exposes life to death.

If you are hovering in some afterlife
    Somewhere in space, you are bound to have seen
Our probes to planets, sent out on behalf
    Of humankind; men soft-land on the moon
For 'all mankind'. It would be a laugh
    If something new evolved beneath the sun
But no: the wars of colour, creed and class;
The same old features on the human face.

What's new? Apart from sensations in science,
    Apart from bigger bombs with bigger bangs,
Apart from ideological alliance
    Between the profit-minded, there are signs
Of something stirring, new malevolence
    Towards the earth itself. Life undermines
The balance of the planet: every year
We add more poison to the atmosphere.

Despite the dangers, intellectuals snooze
    In corners, club-men quietly content:
Philosophers examine the abstruse,
    Their books declare (and show) that nothing's meant
By language; while they mind their ps and qs
    The law is uttered by the government.
Fine minds are closed inside the latest book:
They body-swerve who only sit and look.

It's not enough to merge into the crowd,
　　It's not enough to seek a slick escape,
It's not enough to think your thoughts aloud,
　　It's not enough to vainly live in hope,
It's not enough to shape up for your shroud
　　Before you die, it's not enough to mope.
You have to do, not die, take a position:
You have to move mountains beyond your vision.

'While common men grow ignorantly old'
　　You wrote in *Don Juan* (see Canto Ten):
Such folk see life as through a thick blindfold,
　　I also grieve over these common men.
They never rise from birth, they're bought and sold:
　　They die a death, they do not come again.
Yet 'things can change', I think you will agree:
These common men – and women – might be free.

George Gordon (screw Lord Byron) what you wrote
　　And died for is seen cynically now.
What matters is you wrote it and you fought;
　　Forget the cynics and their sacred cow.
I'm glad you said that you were half a Scot:
　　Your better half's the world's affair. So *ciao*,
I'll take my leave. Forgive me this intrusion.
I promise you I'll act on my conclusion.

Doktor Weitundbreit
JOHN MCGILL

He came unheralded to Mansie Leisk's place on a June afternoon in his
20hp speedboat and his cape and monocle and long black beard, carrying
a small black suitcase that he shook and pointed with as he spoke.

Not two minutes later Tammie Simpson turned up with his knives.
Tammie was the village factotum, slow in his head but a wonder with his
hands. He undertook intricate jobs in carpentry, metalwork, mechanics
and butchery for never more nor less than the price of a half-bottle.
Mansie was scratching his bald spot and trying to find a language the
stranger might understand.

'Du sees, Mr eh ... Mr Vite ... dis boy here's just come dis sem
minute tae butcher de baest tae me.'

The stranger's big eyes widened and the monocle dropped and the
suitcase fell to the ground and his beard seemed to lengthen while his
body shook with a passion that for some seconds could not find words
equal to itself.

'But no, zis is impossible! I sink you don't understand ... ze whole
world I am searching ... since ten years ... last mons in Argentina, zis
mons in Tibet ... and always I sink I have it nearly fount and zen my
dreams zey are on ze grount in pieces broken.' He was trembling with
grief now, and no stage-grief either; Mansie Leisk felt the power of it.
'Until now at last I know ... here, only here in ze norse, only here in ze
Shetland Islands ... are such intelligent sheep to be fount.'

'Aye, weel, I'll grant dee he's a wily aald cratur, but ill-trickit and
traawirt as buggery, and mair straff nor he's worth. So I axed Tammie
here tae ...'

'Mr Leisk, it is impossible, I say.'

Portentous now the voice, and threatening. And as he spoke the
stranger reached into his cloak and brought forth a cascading fistful of
monies and thrust it at Mansie Leisk's mouth. 'Ze black ram must live.
He must live to become ze most famous sheep in history.'

Squinting the length of his nose, Mansie Leisk saw mostly uncouth foreign notes, but among them enough hint of comfortable green and blue to set his ears prickling with suppressed excitement. 'Du can maybe luk by again in de mornin, Tammie,' he said to the butcher.

Tammie Simpson nodded, but stayed. Even his lumpish curiosity was stirred.

'I ask only to spend ze night vis him, here in his own sleeping-place. Ant in ze morning ve begin ze teaching,' the Doktor said.

'Du'll be wantin tae spend de night here, den?' Mansie Leisk asked, in a voice heavy with suspicion and greed.

'Ah, yes. But my bed I make here in ze fielt vis ze ram . . . I don't trouble you even a little piece.'

'Ah, weel, but if du intends tae spend the night here . . .?'

'Of course, of course, I understand, Mr Leisk . . . you vant I should . . .' A further teeming fistful of notes emerged from the draperies.

An eye keener than Tammie Simpson's or less single-minded than Herr Doktor Gottlieb Weitundbreit's might have seen the faintest of pink flushes pass across Mansie Leisk's weatherbeaten cheeks.

'Eh . . . thank you aafil much, Mr . . . Professor . . . eh, hid's an aafil bonnie peerie bit of girse, du kens . . . du'll be careful hoo du lies on hid.'

'Aha, Mr Leisk, tomorrow you neet no more grass. Tomorrow your sheep zey eat ze caviare. Tomorrow your black ram becomes ze vorld's first ant only TALKING SHEEP!'

And he placed his left hand on the mossy top of the dyke and vaulted across to introduce himself to his pupil.

Tammie took his knives home and wrapped them in greased brown paper; the simmer dim fell; and while Herr Doktor Gottlieb Weitundbreit communed with the north wind and exchanged somniloquistic confidences with Tusker the black ram, Mansie Leisk knitted his brows and pondered the exchange rate of the yen.

All next morning he saw nothing of the stranger or of the ram, but pained bleatings and unfathomable electronic bleeps drifted through the heather from somewhere below, near the jetty.

Then, not long after noon, the hills were alive with joyous shouting, and Doktor Weitundbreit was bounding up the slope to the crofthouse door.

'Oh vunder, Mr Leisk,' he said. 'Oh vunder, vunder. Your sheep he is no sheep, he is a *genius!* Consummatum est. In vun day, in vun simple morning, I have taught him to speak. No, no, he does not speak, he *discourses* . . . art, religion, science, politic, metaphysic – he discourses on *anysing!*'

He hopped on the heather, circling Mansie Leisk and clapping him on the shoulders and whooping congratulatory whoops that raised the heads of every nibbling sheep on the hillside. His cape flapped in the breeze until he seemed in some danger of taking instant soaring flight out over the voe.

Then he stopped and was solemn. 'Mr Leisk, I am ze most happy of men, and you are ze most rich.'

Mansie Leisk was notoriously the dourest, most camshious, most straight-laced man in the parish. He had once locked himself in his house for a week, refusing to see or hear any human being, because he thought blind old Mina Johnson had seen him from her house high above the voe when he urinated over the side of his boat. And whenever Mr Taylor the minister harangued the congregation, as ministers do, about the faults and follies of rural life, Mansie Leisk's ears would pinken and he would skulk away at the end of the service, convinced that every shaft had been shot at him and him alone. So it was that despite the promise of rewards beyond his maddest imaginings he baulked at Doktor Weitundbreit's suggestion that he should rap on every door in the parish and announce that the world's first talking sheep would deliver its maiden address in the village hall at seven-thirty that very evening. Not until the Doktor began to quantify, to conjure up hundreds and thousands and millions, did his paranoia at last yield to his cupidity. The Doktor unrolled a ready-printed poster for the village-shop window:

WORLD PREMIERE
THE WORLD'S FIRST AND ONLY
TALKING SHEEP
WILL PERFORM BEFORE THE PUBLIC
IN THE VILLAGE HALL
TONIGHT AT 7.30PM
ADMISSION FREE!

Mansie rolled it up again, tucked it under his arm, and set off, a little sheepishly, on his publicity tour.

The hall was crammed, though it was a fine summer night and there was no lack of undone work at the peats and in the fields. Only Tammie Simpson had not taken his place by seven-thirty. He had a job to finish on Jock Manson's tractor, and a whole flock of discoursing sheep would not have drawn him away from the prospect of a summer night with diesel dripping on his nose.

He commanded a clear enough view of the hall from Jock's field, and in the still June air the sounds of the performance carried easily across the shallow valley of Skimla Burn. He would stroll across, he thought, if things began to sound interesting – down the hill, across the stepping-stones and up the gentle rise on the far side to the hall.

He saw Mansie Leisk and the Doktor climb the steps to the side door that gave on to the stage, the one timorous as a plankwalker, the other almost flying in his eagerness; and behind them, on the end of a stout rope, Tusker the black ram looked as inbiggit as ever, and unabashed by his sudden celebrity. The door closed behind them and the buzz of expectation became a roar of welcome (Tammie Simpson was not one to mark the hint of derision in it, though it was not lost on Mansie Leisk), then a tense silence.

Tammie Simpson rolled on to his back and eased himself under the tractor. Minutes passed; the clink of his spanners echoed across the voe.

When the noise came it was too much, too insistent even for Tammie Simpson to ignore. First, a rising charivari of hoots and jeers and whistles, punctuated by the clang of empty beercans on the stage; then the hall itself seemed to raise a vast indignant shout to the summer sky. Tammie Simpson crawled out and peered across the valley. He saw the stage door open and the Doktor come flapping out – a bat stranded in daylight. He saw the Doktor find his bearings, then flap swiftly down towards the jetty. He saw the main doors burst apart and the hall spewing forth the raging crowd.

This he found interesting. He stood up, wiped his hands on his dungarees, and walked down to the burn and the stepping-stones. Before he had begun climbing the rise, he heard the desperate phut-phut of a starter, then the steady buzz of the speedboat skimming across the voe. And by the time his slow stride had taken him to the hall the furore was at an end (admission had, after all, been free) and the crowd was dispersing homewards, its rage transformed into an almost benign scorn for the abject figure of Mansie Leisk, who stood on the steps of the stage door idiotically clutching the end of the stout rope. Mansie Leisk looked at the friendly vacant face of the handyman, and achieving for the moment something of a tragic grandeur, said, 'The tweester . . . the dirty swindling rascal!'

Then moving off home, and dragging the ill-luckit Tusker viciously behind him, he paused long enough to growl over his shoulder: 'Du'll be coming tae butcher de baest in de mornin, Tammie.'

The buzz of the speedboat was still loud in the silence of the voe. Tammie peered for a time, and at last located the small dark shape of the

Doktor, speeding towards the mainland in his vessel that seemed hardly bigger than himself.

'He's heading straight for de Skerry,' Tammie said to himself, and seconds later he heard the scrunch of fibre-glass on rock and saw the black folds of the Doktor's gown spreading themselves on the waves. He watched for a minute longer – there was nothing else to be done, the Skerry being fully two miles out and all the village boats hauled up on the shore – and saw the Doktor waving the small black suitcase above his head; and he heard him cry out, a clear ringing cry: '*Hilfe! Hilfe! Rette mich! Rette mich! Bin kein gewöhnlicher Mensch, bin ein Genius!*'

The suitcase waved ten, twelve times, then Herr Doktor Gottlieb Weitundbreit and his secrets passed below to gladden the hearts of the lobsters.

In the morning, hardly behind the sun, Tammie Simpson was at the crofthouse door with his knives. Getting no reply to his knock, he pushed the door open, stepped into the lobby and along to the ben room, where he found Mansie Leisk squeezed into the furthest, darkest corner. It was clear even to Tammie, who cared nothing for such things, that he was beginning one of his week-long retreats from the society of men and women. They spoke for just three minutes before Tammie came out, collared Tusker the black ram, and dragged him into the outhouse.

As he stood stridey-legs the beast, his razor-honed knife poised by its jugular vein, he heard it speak, in a voice trembling with the fear of death, but nonetheless as clear as Mr Taylor's announcing the hymns on Sunday: '*Hilfe! Hilfe! Rette mich! Rette mich! Bin kein gewöhnliches Schaf, bin ein Genius!*'

He hesitated for a second, then comfortably drew the blade across the pulsing throat. He watched the blood spurt, and shook his head and said aloud to himself the words he had just heard from Mansie Leisk: 'Whit bluidy use is a sheep that canna spik Shetland?'

The Gift

(Thomas of Ercildoune was a makar and a singer. He was visited by the Queen of Elfland. But instead
of a song, she left him the gift of truth like a pebble in his mouth)

RODERICK WATSON

1

When I played the flute for you in the green domain
of braes and stones   I made long tunes
with subtle cadence and measure of my breath
going out   (Ragas   on larochs
at the head of a glen where three burns meet)
ahhhh   breath like water over moss
so endlessly   leaving: I did not know . . .
I did not know that you would come to me.

To mind: or rise to the intricate strain
unwinding on your face (spools and thread
and asphodel in the passage of the tune
silver bells in the air   the roar of the sea
velvet   salt   the taste of blood)
yes   turns without end   yes   and I
playing like some staggered stirk before your grace
(yes) to keep the present   from getting away.

You dance   so slowly.   Contained in frozen steps
a foot held high   to turn at the calm water
and cross the lintel in the grass   one arm
to rise   and slowly as a flower is slow
to reach the neck   bend the wrist
and open very slowly your hand (like an eye!)
so.   Lean my head upon your knee   so
I remember   remember me.

Now by the mill-town I remain
and tumbled lime-kilns at my foot
the ground broken   no breath for the flute
or the tunes I hear   and no words come
but ash and rubbish of the truth   well . . .
(the lime was used to put upon the land
it was made by burning stones
though not any more as you can see)

well . . . now the bracken is rusting everywhere
(O lady return   and set me free).

2

He walked the city between the walls
of tenements   narrow wynds and old close steps
became a scholar of escarpments: boarded windows
cobbled streets and iron spears repaired with wire
for he was sure the dance was there
lines of a reel he could not read
on flaked and cracked eroding stone.
He did not see her name.

Later he learned the gift on the walls
and it said
Keep the Pope off the blue moon
Fuck the Scots Forever
Lick it and see
TRUE

3

'In the evening the company danced as usual. We performed, with much activity, a dance which, I suppose, the emigration from Skye has occasioned. They call it America. Each of the couples, after the common *involutions* and *evolutions*, successively whirls round in a circle, till all are in motion; and the dance seems intended to show how emigration catches, till a whole neighbourhood is set afloat. Mrs M'Kinnon told me, that last year, when a ship sailed from Portree for America, the people on shore were almost distracted when they saw their relations go off; they lay down on the ground, tumbled, and tore the grass with their teeth. This year there was not a tear shed. The people on the shore seemed to think that they would soon follow.'

Tour of the Hebrides

4

Once between drinks   between jokes
I bought a rattle from a ragged man
– crown tops in a wicker cage –
before the barman drove him out
with his stick and his coat and his tartan tam'
gas-mask case and a 'Rangers' bag.
The retreat from Culloden.
Salt-stained boots at the Somme.
The month it was May and the lilacs smelled sweet
I was strolling one evening round town . . .
His name was MacCrimmon.

Later I threw the rattle away   for
who would give it to a child?

MacCrimmon used to walk among the Meadows.

5

Als I me went this endris day
        Full fast in mind makkand my moan,
In the merry morning of May
        By Huntly Bankis myself alone,

I heard the jay and the throstell,
        The mavis menied of her sang,
The woodwale beried als a bel,
        That all the wood about me rang.

Alone in longing, thus als I lay,
        Underneith a seemly tree,
Saw I quhare a lady gay
        Came ridand ower a lang lee.

If I suld sit to Doomisday
        With my tongue to wrob and wrye,
Certainly that lady gay
        Never be she described by me.

6
RHYMER

Let's say the sky is 'blue'
It's not enough to catch the space
The true emptiness above the hill
Cold   clear   shrill   high
The eggshell grace of the winter sky.

Call the hillside 'brown' and 'green'
'Grey' stone and 'black' earth
But words will never say the scene
The clean rock   its depth   its mass
And the yellow death of the hillside grass.
Water.   Mist.   Space.   White light.
How long to here?   ·

Peat water is brackish brown
like tea (write it down) and
heather root is silver ash   old
tough   sharp   cold.

To walk miles on broken stones
a hollow path in the bones of the glen.

To rest on a bank (True Thomas)
and to miss her   after years
a face in the pool   a high pass
the wind in the rigging of the hills.

Water.   Mist.   Space.   White light.
And how long?   Lying here?

Let's say the sky is 'blue'
It's not enough to catch the space
The true emptiness above the hill
Cold   clear   shrill   high
The eggshell grace of the winter sky.

Call the hillside 'brown' and 'green'
'Grey' stone and 'black' earth

But words will never say the scene
The clean rock   its depth   its mass
And the yellow death of the hillside grass.

7

Alone in longing as I lay.
Recalled
cold mornings in the park and
the mavis in her song:
at the green pavilion

the sound of water on the tiles
all night   going away

– the lintel in the grass
where the hearth stones sank
like islands in the sea

– the cardboard shelter
in bushes by the golfcourse.

In the evening
the company danced as usual.

I drank the cup of bitter wine
For well we knew the fault was mine
   And I went the way I came.

They call it America.

8

THE PRESENT

Loss or a sense of loss: it comes to mind
distant as passion in the stone
(the dance within the pebble)
or when my son pressed his brow
into my cheek with the fiercest wish
of bone to be one with bone.

Or late at night   distracted   mean
and restless with the radio on
stars on stars   light years stream
above us at the bottom of a well
longing   longing will find its scene
AFN   208   the Late Late Show
(a treacle well) Oh Alice!   Oh eighteen!

Later (since you) days opened as simply
as a door: standing on the flint floor
of Tuscany watching light like a tower
across a valley of olives   and vines
and dust.   Or on the shore at Ord when
we laid out fishbox ends to spell
our names: Ullapool   Hull
Lochinver   Stonehaven. Good times.

Tonight he slips between us in the bed
and sticks his feet into my ribs.
I hear him snuffle in his sleep.
(I have so much) and you
are restless with another life
so: we are all here (light years
Alice   and old rocks to keep).

Outside   the lamps turn our quiet street
to ice. I lie and count
flashes of fire   in the darkness
of the roof (you give so much)
'These are rods and cones' I say . . .
but the present . . . like sparks . . . getting away.

Vigil

TOM HUBBARD

The April of the great frost:
We were seized, tied, freeze-dried paper-thin
Like headlines blowing, *Come the morn, we'll win:*
– Or lose, perhaps, with fingers double-crossed.

The daft auld limmer shivers on the hill:
She has nae flair, her bairns hae kest her oot;
– Time wis, fowk said 'We'll keep ye, hen, fae the chill.
We'll rost ye ti a bing o banes an soot!'

Aiblins the day she's feart ti meet thae tykes
That huddle roun the burner endlessly:
'Come, mither, jyne us at the guairdit dykes:
They've locked the door an bunged awa the key.'

Her voice (the tykes said) wis nae carlin's speak:
A young-like lassie on the road, aamaist.
They watched her beauty vanish i the reek
– Wis she a wumman, thon, or else a ghaist?

The Saltire flies over St Andrew's House.
There's a fireworks on MacDiarmid Boulevard.
Republic Day's a carnival carouse
As Scottish men try hard not to be hard.

'Course, it's a game, just. Harmless way to rest.
It makes a change from fitbaa, and that's good.
The Scottish Secretary's fair impressed;
It's doubtful, though, if he has understood.

When Czechs have sung 'Where is my home?'
We'll grunt 'No dosh? – No room at the inn!'
We'll sell the Euros a kilted gnome
With a pawky wee North-British grin.

He'll come complete with his but-and-ben
(A Scotsman's home is not a castle)
And his deferential vote, ye ken,
Eliminating any hassle.

What, flower of Scotland? Terrace-stuff!
Election night, we know who's boss.
Don't come it with that soulful guff:
Most of us couldn't give a toss.

Oor gnome's the ideal Embro guide:
At culture, too, he's maist kenspeckle;
Although he looks like Mr Hyde,
He'd more than pass for Dr Jekyll.

Oor intelligentsia? Puir sowls,
Pontification throu their bowels;
Postmodernism's pic 'n' mix
Is aa their intellectual kicks.

Scotland's cultural independence
Is clear to anyone who looks:
– They've taen folk's cairdboard boxes awa,
Recycled thaim inti poetry buiks.

They've smothered sexuality
With jargonfriendly, fake polemics:
Intertextuality
Between consenting academics.

Aince makars sang it rare an roch –
Their darg wis clear, sans doobt,
No ti poure honey in the troch
But cowp the damn thing oot.

We're saved bi the *amadan naomh*, the haly fool;
La Mancha's on the Calton; Prof. Miguel
De Unamuno praised Don Quixote's rule –
Ti lowp wi faith abune the rational.

Travelling homefully – biding to arrive –
You'll recognise a folk from where they've dossed.
How can a gangrel few remain alive?
They, who have not betrayed, have surely lost?

GLOSSARY

limmer	woman	*aince*	once
flair	floor	*makars*	poets
rost	roast	*roch*	rough
bing	heap	*darg*	task
aiblins	perhaps	*troch*	trough
dykes	walls	*cowp*	overturn
carlin	old woman	*amadan naomdh* (Gaelic)	holy fool
on the road	pregnant		
kenspeckle	conspicuous	*lowp*	leap
puir sowls	poor souls	*gangrel*	vagabond

Requiem:

Thirteen Lucky Poems

WALTER PERRIE

You, sometimes, will lament a lost friend,
For it is a custom:
This care for past men . . .

Ezra Pound
Homage to Sextus Propertius

DEPARTURE I

Failing lovers
drinkers at dawn
cafés
under this tyranny
these unacknowledged
vanishings
stumble
one by one
signlike
towards vacancy.

RETURN I

Though frost through five
nights has thickened its gelid crust
the burn swings on
shadowy minnows a-flitter
in unison.

Hot coffee by the hissing fire
and the bland voice exhausting dire
events across four continents;
how many died, how many may expire.

Biscuit-dry crisp
hills under snowy icing
and ptarmigan
crackle and yap, whurr from the sight
of the human.

Read Hume *On Miracles* again.
Misanthropy is easy when
abstraction and unloving fact
extract the love-lost citizen.

On the high tops
in the deep deer-sheltering glens
weak things totter
and the hungry dipper baffled
walks on water.

DEPARTURE II

Fine-grained as though duration
were density the image
records each light-carved detail:
legendary doors ajar
and inter-twining angels
tenth-century bishops
gargoyle heads, early Saints –
who may have existed or not.
As though duration were density
in extended exposure
the flitting crowds have gone.

RETURN II

Presence why do you hide so
for ever skip hopping
from word to word your cuckoo
calling always stopping
when I think I have you?

Why so wilfully obscure?
Is it a con, a shame
at some wound or want in our
tryst – or a stupid game
without meaning or cure?

Or do I slyly exile
you fearfully greedy
for some phantasy to wile
out death ever needy
of new woods, another style?

Whimsical as a cuckoo
you vanish for days, years
till, all at once, peek-a-boo
you assaulting my ears.
Presence why do you hide so?

Presence, Presence have I guessed
how you find your victim's nest –
between hope and hurt a secret place
thorny as life and thin as grace?

DEPARTURE III
(*After* Hokusai)

Skewed line of the ruled pine
leaning back from an edge
hides a triangular
terror – pine, rider, horse
poised upon emptiness.

Where we have paused to look
there is nothing to see
nothing below our crag
but purple abyss and
celebratory snow.

The horse bows down his head
knowing the rider's face
is turned away too tired
of the poems he can
not love or abandon.

Sound souls asleep in
dry taciturn houses
we are abandoned by
will not miss us. Morning
will not have covered our tracks.

Rider and horse withdraw
from sadness to go on
fording white spaces where
we may not follow them
through their maidenly snow.

RETURN III

Dominican
peeweeps
sweeten
their earth again.

Oyster-catchers
beat a piercing
way up river and in
the guttering
snowmelt
morning
a pair of sparrows
polkas.

Foam-fingered
greedily
green waves
reach
for me
and the dragon
thin with dancing
high above
remembered
mountains.

RETURN IV

Through plum
stain windows
sun sweet
plovers
rise from foam.
What is there not
to celebrate?

DEPARTURE V (*traditional*)

By the balcony
        The moon is out
my friend looks back
        for hearts fishing
to invisible homes
        boats are leaving
forbidden
        harbour and pine
exile
        is gripping earth
loss
        hard
and far away.

RETURN V

The small rain settles in to Creag nan Gabhar
drawing the skies down, stirring the ember
moss to brightness, hitching the faded haar
        more tightly to her shoulders
    till from the cloud and drowsing boulders
        nine regal does come trotting
down, indian-file to their peat-black pool
and wait, alert, immobile, undrinking.
Unmoving I wait breathing slowly, wait
        crouched in the heather, sodden
    chilled. The curlews are silenced, the spate
of the earth-brown burn inaudible.
    What are we waiting for? But still they
        wait till the hillside shivers
    numbly forgetting to exhale.
    Then, I see, half-see him through the haar
albino stag almost invisible.

DEPARTURE VI

    artless armoured
    innocents mortal
    we
    adventured out
    to track
    down dragonish
    mystery

    our selves
    stalked stalled
    capricious
    you solo
    precede me

blatant now
the facts
of being
conscious
physical
going to die
are more
than mystery
enough

TENEBRAE

The once umbilical places severed
look littler now than remembered confusing
loftier eyes with unmeaning loss.
The stones are stones and sward and whin
disguise themselves behind loneliness.
No man steps in the same stream twice.
Questing waters trickle or spate at flaw
and crack in the widening sense of limit
as the silt in the heart's channel shifts.
We are not large enough to contain our dying.
Smoother, lighter than any liquid
it assumes our shaping sadness to define
all we failed in becoming as goal
and origin exclude all but skeletal
prehension.

A tense imperfect is our tributary
glossing our glories out over the lip
of a fall out into prismatic light.
Whatever provocation flaw and foible
can solicit from nothing kneads us
moulding their definite conduit and course
hurtless as the gift of pain. What we are
good at is suffering, not on behalf
of anything but quantum by quantum

inventing loss unthinking why the heart
behaves so badly. None of our numbers
count what we inflict on water nor tongues
name what we foil and foul. What's given
only osmoses back into earth-stuff
and silence.

Thinking of you now and all we were not
I should put out honey and oatbree
to sweeten the throats of our shadows.
This is no place for forgiveness their thirst
has still to be sated and we to become
selflessly fluent in otherness.
O spirits help us to bear the straining
syntax of water shape-shifting as
with absolute authority autumn
places a blue spear straight through the heart.
The easy part is the resigning
art of tumbling into the letterless
blue far out and high above the wrinkling shore
where sea and sun circle as eagles and
soar soar soar.

KELLS

praise on praise
curlicue forest
faces peer from
page on page
labours asleep
like seed o
in bird woven
branches bold
with berries
calling
to morning
translate me

eat me out
of this marriage
to old skins
better abandoned

angel and animal
stacked
in our stories
wait for
a reader
patient
to flutter and stump
from crypts where scripts
are encrypted
from cells
to suns
drunk over
an O or the L
of a bell
summoning
lover